# CliffsNotes™

# Aeneid

**By Richard McDougall, PhD.**
**and Suzanne Pavlos, M. Ed.**

## IN THIS BOOK

- Discover Virgil and his writing
- Preview an Introduction to the Poem
- Explore themes, character development, and recurring images in the Critical Commentaries
- Savor in-depth Character Analyses
- Acquire an understanding of the poem with Critical Essays
- Reinforce what you learn with CliffsNotes Review
- Find additional information to further your study in CliffsNotes Resource Center and online at www.cliffsnotes.com

WILEY
Wiley Publishing, Inc.

**About the Author**
Suzanne Pavlos, a former high school teacher, currently works as a freelance writer and editor. Suzanne is also a certified social worker and is currently completing a residency in psychotherapy.

**Publisher's Acknowledgments**
*Editorial*
Project Editor: Alissa D. Cayton
Acquisitions Editor: Greg Tubach
Copy Editor: Rowena Rappaport
Glossary Editors: The editors and staff at Webster's New World™ Dictionaries
Editorial Administrator: Michelle Hacker
Editorial Assistant: Jennifer Young
*Composition*
Indexer: York Production Services, Inc.
Proofreader: York Production Services, Inc.
Wiley Indianapolis Composition Services

CliffsNotes™ *Aeneid*

Published by
Wiley Publishing, Inc.
111 River Street
Hoboken, NJ 07030
www.wiley.com

Copyright © 2001 Wiley Publishing, Inc., New York, New York
Library of Congress Control Number: 00-107700
ISBN: 0-7645-8680-7
Printed in the United States of America
10 9 8 7
1O/TR/QT/QX/IN
Published by Wiley Publishing, Inc., New York, NY
Published simultaneously in Canada

# Table of Contents

# How to Use This Book

This CliffsNotes study guide on Virgil's *Aeneid* supplements the original literary work, giving you background information about the author, an introduction to the work, a graphical character map, critical commentaries, expanded glossaries, and a comprehensive index, all for you to use as an educational tool that will allow you to better understand *Aeneid*. This study guide was written with the assumption that you have read *Aeneid*. Reading a literary work doesn't mean that you immediately grasp the major themes and devices used by the author; this study guide will help supplement your reading to be sure you get all you can from Virgil's *Aeneid*. CliffsNotes Review tests your comprehension of the original text and reinforces learning with questions and answers, practice projects, and more. For further information on Virgil and *Aeneid*, check out the CliffsNotes Resource Center.

CliffsNotes provides the following icons to highlight essential elements of particular interest:

Reveals the underlying themes in the work.

Helps you to more easily relate to or discover the depth of a character.

Uncovers elements such as setting, atmosphere, mystery, passion, violence, irony, symbolism, tragedy, foreshadowing, and satire.

Enables you to appreciate the nuances of words and phrases.

## Don't Miss Our Web Site

Discover classic literature as well as modern-day treasures by visiting the CliffsNotes Web site at www.cliffsnotes.com. You can obtain a quick download of a CliffsNotes title, purchase a title in print form, browse our catalog, or view online samples.

You'll also find interactive tools that are fun and informative, links to interesting Web sites, tips, articles, and additional resources to help you, not only for literature, but for test prep, finance, careers, computers, and Internet too. See you at www.cliffsnotes.com!

# LIFE AND BACKGROUND OF THE POET

The following abbreviated biography of Publius Vergilius Maro is provided so that you might become more familiar with his life and the historical times that possibly influenced his writing. Read this Life and Background of the Author section and recall it when reading Virgil's *Aeneid*, thinking of any thematic relationship between Virgil's work and his life.

# Personal Background

Publius Vergilius Maro was born October 15, 70 B.C., in the northern Italian village of Andes, a town just outside the city of Mantova, known today as Mantua. Although his name is correctly spelled "Vergil," the variant "Virgil" is more commonly used. This name derives from the Latin word *virga*, meaning "wand," which reflects the belief, prevalent during the Middle Ages, that a poet is a great magician, with the power to conjure dead spirits.

The eldest of three sons—his brother Silo died in childbirth, and Flaccus, his other brother, lived only to young manhood—Virgil came from a prosperous family. His father, an industrious potter and cattle farmer, married his landlord's daughter, worked at beekeeping, and invested in the lumber industry. An ambitious man, he strove to provide Virgil with an aristocratic education to prepare him for a law career.

# Education

Virgil attended school in Cremona and then, briefly, in Milan. In 54 or 53 B.C., he went to Rome, where he studied law and rhetoric in the school, or academy, of Epidius. There, he met Octavian, a fellow student, who, as the future emperor Augustus, would become Virgil's patron. Virgil had intended to become a lawyer as his father wished, but after arguing his first law case he turned to the study of philosophy, finding it more congenial to his temperament.

# Early Works

In 49 B.C., the year Julius Caesar crossed the Rubicon River with his legions of soldiers and marched on Rome to seize power, Virgil, to escape the civil disturbances that Caesar's arrival created, left the city and moved to Naples. There, he studied with the philosopher Siro. It is uncertain whether a number of minor poems attributed to Virgil, including "Culex" ("The Gnat"), "Copa" ("The Barmaid"), and "Catalepton" ("Trifles"), were written by him, but if so, some of them may have been completed at this time.

After Caesar's assassination in 44 B.C., Virgil returned to Mantova, where, a year later, he began the composition of his first important work, a collection of ten poems known as the *Eclogues*, or "Selections," sometimes called the *Bucolics*, or "Pastoral Poems." Published in 37 B.C., the

*Eclogues* depict the lives and loves of shepherds in idealized rural settings. However, the first and ninth *Eclogues*, which are more realistic than the others, allude to the politically motivated confiscation of Mantuan farms, which were awarded to war veterans after the forces of Octavian, Lepidus, and Mark Antony defeated Brutus's and Cassius's armies at the Battle of Philippi in 42 B.C. When his father's estate was confiscated in 41 B.C., Virgil appealed to Octavian for restitution, although there is considerable uncertainty and disagreement as to the result of this appeal. The confiscated property may have been regained, or, failing that, residences in Rome and Naples may have been awarded to him as compensation for the loss of his patrimony.

With the publication of the *Eclogues*, Virgil achieved great popular success. By this time, he had reestablished his friendship with Octavian and had met Maecenas, the future emperor's wealthy and powerful advisor, whose house was a gathering place for poets and other men of letters. This acquaintance no doubt influenced Virgil's *Georgics*, which was his second and final important work before he began writing the *Aeneid*.

Virgil undertook the *Georgics* not long after the publication of the *Eclogues*. A didactic poem of over two thousand lines, the *Georgics* ("About Farming") was completed in 30 B.C., after seven years of labor, during which time Virgil lived chiefly in Naples, the city he loved most. On one level, this work, in four books, is about animal husbandry and agricultural methods, topics that might have been suggested by Maecenas, to whom the poem is dedicated, and who was interested in reviving farming as a way of life for war veterans. On a deeper level, the *Georgics* celebrates the beauty and power of nature and stresses the importance of living in harmony with it. It also contains references to the future emperor Augustus and the peace his reign promises after years of civil war.

## The Writing of the *Aeneid*

The *Aeneid*, Rome's national epic and one of the literary master-pieces of Western civilization, was begun in 30 B.C., and all of Rome, and especially the royal court, followed its progress. As he refined this work during his later years, Virgil led a comfortable, worry-free life, devoting himself to historical research for the *Aeneid* and enjoying the luxuries that his father's bequest and the emperor's patronage provided. Especially encouraged by Augustus, to whom the poem is dedicated, he worked on the epic exclusively until his untimely death eleven years later, when the poem was substantially finished but lacked the final polish that, as a perfectionist, Virgil had hoped to give it.

Virgil had planned to spend three years in Greece and Asia revising the *Aeneid* while visiting the sites it mentions. He got as far as Athens, where he met Augustus, who, returning from a visit to the island of Samos, persuaded the poet to accompany him to Italy. Already in declining health, Virgil became severely ill en route and died in Brundisium— modern Brindisi—on September 21, 19 B.C., close to his fifty-first birthday. On his deathbed, he reportedly composed a short, subtle epitaph for himself, which his friends inscribed on his now-vanished tomb in Naples: "Mantua me genuit; Calabri rapuere; tenet nunc Parthenope; cecini pascua, rura, duces." The epitaph, which translates as "Mantua gave me birth, Calabria took me away, and now Naples holds me; I sang of pastures, farms, leaders," summarizes Virgil's three great works, which chronicle the history of Rome, from shepherds to farmers to soldiers.

Shortly before his death, Virgil requested that the *Aeneid* manuscript be destroyed, as he did not want to leave it in its unfinished state, but Augustus, mindful of the genius of a work that would long outlive the passing of his empire, wisely countermanded the poet's wish. The emperor assigned two of Virgil's friends, Varius Rufus and Plotius Tucca, to edit the manuscript for publication, but he cautioned them not to make any poetic additions. The work, completed near the end of 18 B.C., achieved immediate acceptance throughout the Mediterranean world as the definitive Roman epic.

# Preserving the *Aeneid* through the Centuries

Three manuscripts of the *Aeneid* from the fourth and fifth centuries are the basis of the text of the poem in use today. Surprisingly, these manuscripts are relatively free from mistakes and generally agree with one another—evidence that the scribes who reproduced them were working with consistently good, earlier copies of the poem, which had to be painstakingly copied again and again by hand, a method that invited error.

It was the custom when composing by hand, as Virgil did, to write on tablets coated with wax. The text was etched into the wax surface by means of a stylus, an instrument with a sharp point at one end and a flat edge, used for erasing, at the other. Later, professional copyists, using a primitive pen and ink, transcribed the individual books of the *Aeneid* onto papyrus, a form of paper made from the papyrus plant. The papyrus sheets were then glued together and rolled into a scroll. The reader would hold the scroll in one hand and unwind it with the other onto another spool, a very unwieldy method.

After Virgil's death, the *Aeneid* magnified his fame. It was studied in schools, and numerous biographies of the poet were written—a sure sign of popular interest. The earliest and longest of these, dating from the fourth century, is by the grammarian Aelius Donatus, whose source of information was a lost *Life of Virgil* by the Roman historian Suetonius, who is best known for his *Lives of the Caesars*, about the first twelve Roman emperors.

Around the end of the fifth century, Ambrosius Macrobius, another grammarian, composed a dialogue called *Saturnalia*, in which guests at a fictional dinner party discuss the *Aeneid*. The dialogue offers a picture of Rome's cultured pagan society as it was just before it became Christian. Among the guests at the dinner is a professor named Servius, who in real life wrote a commentary on the *Aeneid* that, in spite of factual errors, has been a valuable source of information for later scholars.

Following Rome's conversion to Christianity, Virgil continued to be highly regarded. During the Middle Ages, he was thought to have had "a naturally Christian soul"—the conventional expression used to identify a person who, it was believed, would have embraced Christianity but for the accident of having been born before Christ. This conviction was based on the evidence of Virgil's compassionate nature, which is manifested throughout the *Aeneid*, and on the belief that Virgil had foretold the coming of Christ in the fourth *Eclogue*, in which he prophesies a golden age of peace and good will ushered in by the birth of a divine child. He also became the subject of many legends that obscured his real importance as a poet by featuring him as a magician with supernatural powers. Still, his works continued to be read; even people who abhorred Rome's former worship of Jupiter, Minerva, and other pagan gods used Virgil's texts to teach Latin grammar and style.

During the European Renaissance—roughly, the 1500s to the 1700s, an era marked by a rebirth of interest in classical art, learning, and literature—both Greek and Roman writers were fervently admired and imitated. Knowledge of the Greek language, which had been lost during the Middle Ages, was once more available. Homer was again read in the original, and Virgil was increasingly and universally admired.

The eighteenth century was one that especially esteemed elegance and artifice, and so Virgil was prized. However, under the influence of romanticism, which came toward the end of the century and prevailed in the first part of the next, there was a change in critical standards. Enthusiasm and the free expression of individual feelings were prized by Keats, Shelley, Byron, Wordsworth, and Coleridge—the great poets of this era, and all radically different in spirit from Virgil. For these romanticists, Aeneas represented the hero who favors the founding of a state over the more important goals of personal happiness and fulfillment.

The *Aeneid* continues to be read today for two main reasons. The first is that, like all successful poets, Virgil expresses in powerful and beautiful language the humanity that we share with him over the centuries that separate us. The second reason why the *Aeneid* continues to be read is that, along with other Roman writings and achievements, it forms a priceless part of the cultural heritage of modern Western civilization. Although the events described in the epic belong far more to the realm of myth and legend than to actual history, the poem gives us, for that very reason, an idealized picture of the way a great people wished to see themselves and their place in the world. Our understanding of their aspirations adds to our knowledge of our past.

The *Aeneid*, then, in addition to appealing to us as a timeless work of literature, also has a documentary interest for present-day readers. In this light, it can be seen as an attempt to inculcate in its first readers a reverence for the history of the Roman Empire and a love for traditional Roman virtues and for Rome itself. Many of the laws and customs that were so prized by Romans remain our own, and other achievements of Rome continue to affect us as well. For example, Roman architecture, derived from Greek models but made more daringly massive and imposing because of Roman engineering genius, influenced the style of edifices that have followed down to our own time. Perhaps most important, Latin, in which the *Aeneid* was written, is the foundation of the modern romance languages—notably French, Spanish, and Italian—now spoken in the countries that occupy the regions that were once part of the Roman Empire, and from which the English language is also derived.

While we cannot approach the epic poem in the patriotic fervor of its first readers, for whom it was a national epic intended to glorify Rome's power and destiny, the adventures of Aeneas and his followers, who go in search of a new homeland after the Greeks's destruction of Troy, continue to interest us because they appeal to our basic human desire to believe in a meaningful world watched over and directed by a divine providence, in which heroic perseverance is finally rewarded.

# INTRODUCTION TO THE POEM

The following Introduction section is provided solely as an educational tool and is not meant to replace the experience of your reading the work. Read the Introduction and A Brief Synopsis to enhance your understanding of the work and to prepare yourself for the critical thinking that should take place whenever you read any work of fiction or nonfiction. Keep the List of Characters and Character Map at hand so that as you read the original literary work, if you encounter a character about whom you're uncertain, you can refer to the List of Characters and Character Map to refresh your memory.

# Introduction

The *Aeneid*, the story of a band of survivors who leave their destroyed city to seek another home in a faraway country, is about rebirth, about life springing forth from ruin and death. It is primarily a fiction whose narrative fabric, woven from myth and legend, traces a pattern that appears in the most profound myths that concern the human spirit's eternal quest for self-perpetuation. We must bear in mind, however, that the epic was seen in an entirely different light by Virgil's contemporaries. Because the events that take place in the poem were recounted from generation to generation, they eventually took on the appearance of unquestionable truth.

Long before Virgil's time, Romans liked to believe that among their ancestors were the legendary Trojans, who, under Aeneas's leadership, sailed from Troy, in Asia Minor (present-day Turkey), westward across the Mediterranean Sea to Italy and settled in Latium, site of the future Rome. This legend of Aeneas's voyage, which the Romans elaborated for their own patriotic purposes, was recorded as far back as the fifth century B.C. by a Greek, Hellenicus of Lesbos. In the following century, another Greek, Timaeus, told how Aeneas established the city of Lavinium, which is referred to at the very beginning of the *Aeneid*.

According to Roman legend, Rome itself was founded in 753 B.C. by one of Aeneas's descendants, Romulus, who, with his twin brother, Remus, was a son of Mars, the god of war, and the Vestal Virgin Rhea Silvia. To account for the gap in time between the date of the fall of Troy, which a Roman historian fixed at 1184 B.C., and the date of the city's founding, it was imagined that several generations of kings had intervened between these two dates, including Aeneas's son, Ascanius— also known as Iulus—and Numitor, the grandfather of Romulus and Remus.

In fact, the Romans were descended from Indo-European tribes that came southward over the Alps into Italy perhaps as long ago as the middle of the second millennium B.C. Rome, while it had begun to exist in the century assigned by legend, was initially a confederation of shepherd villages. Until 509 B.C., this coalition of villages was ruled by kings, some of whom were Etruscans, members of a tribe who supposedly came from Asia Minor, as the legendary Trojans were supposed to have done. In 509 B.C., however, when the last Etruscan king, Tarquin the Proud, was deposed and Rome became a republic, the Etruscans were vanquished, and thereafter their power waned. In the *Aeneid*,

Etruscan warriors, rebelling against their evil king, Mezentius, fight on the side of the Trojans in their war against the Latins.

This instance of a real people who played a real role in the early development of Rome, fighting in a war that can only be regarded as essentially fictitious, offers an example of how legend and history could easily coexist in the Roman mind. Virgil probably assumed that his contemporary readers would regard the primary legends of their national origins, those surrounding Aeneas, as true, and that they would recall Book XX of Homer's *Iliad*, in which Aeneas, after boasting of his illustrious lineage to Achilles and then engaging in combat against this greatest of Greek warriors, is rescued from certain death by the sea god Poseidon—the Roman Neptune—because it had been prophesied that Aeneas would be the leader of the Trojan survivors.

Not only Greek literature but Greek religion, as well, was familiar to the Romans, who, during the third and second centuries B.C., merged it with their own, identifying Italian divinities with Greek counterparts to the point of regarding the latter as being the same ones except under different, Greek names. Virgil's contemporary readers were thoroughly acquainted with the personalities and doings of the gods and goddesses, who generate so much of the action of the Trojan War and provide the vital force of so many other Greek legends and myths.

Therefore, when Virgil, in the opening section of the *Aeneid*, cites the "judgment Paris gave"—the *judicium Paridis*, in Latin—as a reason for Juno's implacable hatred of the Trojans, his readers would have understood immediately this wonderfully succinct allusion, which helped explain why Juno, the queen of the gods, would be a formidable opponent throughout the epic poem. Paris's judgment, which concerned the awarding of a golden apple—the prize in a kind of divine beauty contest presided over by Paris, a son of Troy's King Priam and Queen Hecuba—led to the Trojan War and so to the downfall of Troy and, by extension, to Rome's founding.

The golden apple, with its inscription, "For the Fairest," was in itself a trifle, but it produced such far-reaching effects because it acted as a stimulus to the passions of humans and immortals alike. Angered because she had not been invited to a wedding, Eris, the goddess of discord, tossed the apple among the assembled guests, setting off a controversy among three goddesses who were present: Venus, the goddess of love; Juno, the queen of the gods; and Minerva, the goddess of wisdom, each of whom believed that the inscription on the apple could refer only to herself.

Paris, who had been appointed by Jupiter to pronounce judgment in the matter, awarded the apple to Venus, who in return for this favor promised him the most beautiful woman in the world, a reward that he, reputed to be the most handsome man in the world, valued more than those offered by Juno and Minerva—worldly power and victory in war, respectively. Juno took Paris's judgment as a personal insult that wounded her vanity and aggravated a deep-seated antagonism, for she knew that her favorite city, Carthage, was destined to be razed by Rome and its citizens sold into slavery.

The woman Paris won was Helen, the wife of the Greek Menelaus, king of Sparta. When Paris and Helen eloped, Menelaus attempted peacefully to have her returned to him. However, when these attempts failed, he and his brother, Agamemnon, king of Mycenae, assembled a fleet of a thousand ships and an enormous army, and the war against Troy began.

The bitter hatred that existed between the Greeks and the Trojans seemed too great for Virgil to explain without including a supernatural reason for it. His contemporary readers would have been certain that when, in Book IV, Queen Dido of Carthage curses the Trojans and calls for a hero to avenge Aeneas's abandoning her, she is referring unwittingly to the great Carthaginian general Hannibal, who with his warriors and elephants laid waste to Italy for more than fourteen years during the Second Punic War. In all, there were three Punic Wars between Carthage and Rome: the First Punic War (264–241 B.C.), the Second Punic War (218–201 B.C.), and the Third Punic War (149–146 B.C.), which ended with Carthage's destruction. For Virgil's readers, all three of these wars would have seemed like the fulfillment, in far later times, of Dido's curse.

In the years that followed Carthage's destruction, Rome waged war victoriously against foreign powers that stood in the way of her irresistible drive toward domination, notably kingdoms that had been parts of Alexander the Great's empire: Syria, Macedonia, and Egypt. The wars against Macedonia, four in all, finally brought Greece under Rome's complete control.

These wars vastly increased Rome's power and wealth, but at home the republic entered a period of civil disorder to which many causes have been assigned. These include inflation; the monopoly of agriculture by wealthy landowners to the detriment of small farmers; the clamor for Roman citizenship by Italians who were not Romans; the devastation of Italy during the Second Punic War; the corruption of the governors of new provinces; and, most important, the very expansion of Rome, which changed from a small city-state into an empire that was too large to be administered by the old republican type of government in which two consuls, elected every year, wielded power between them, each having the right to veto the other's decisions.

In the final days of the Roman republic, a series of ambitious and brutal leaders struggled for control of the state, but none was able to solve Rome's problems or establish lasting power for himself and his faction of supporters. Among these would-be rulers were the three members of the First Triumvirate, Crassus, Pompey, and Julius Caesar, who in 49 B.C. marched on Rome with his legions and in the following year defeated Pompey, who had become his rival; and the Second Triumvirate of Mark Antony, Lepidus, and Octavian, who finally gained power for himself in 31 B.C. after defeating the combined forces of Antony and Cleopatra, Egypt's queen, at the Battle of Actium.

Octavian, Rome's first emperor, whom the Roman Senate officially named Augustus—meaning "revered"—in 27 B.C., had been as unscrupulous and cruel as any of the other power seekers while consolidating his position. Able to bring order where other leaders had failed, he reorganized the Roman bureaucracy and opened its membership to common men, freedmen, and even slaves. He cleverly masked his power, which was absolute, by retaining the old forms of republican government.

Virgil, who came to maturity as a poet while the republic was in its death throes, longed for the peace that Augustus promised and eventually brought, and supported wholeheartedly the emperor's policies. The simultaneous appearance of these two figures on the world's stage— the man of power able to inspire the man of poetic genius—resulted in the *Aeneid*, whose primary purpose was to remind its original readers of the heroic past from which Rome was believed to have sprung, and to arouse hopes for an equally heroic future.

(All quotations are from Robert Fitzgerald's translation, *The Aeneid*, published by Random House, 1983.)

# A Brief Synopsis

The Trojans have just set sail from Sicily on the last leg of their voyage to Italy when the goddess Juno commands Aeolus, god of the winds, to raise a storm, which drives the Trojan fleet to the coast of Libya, site of Carthage. Dido, the city's ruler, welcomes them. She gives a banquet in honor of their leader, Aeneas, at which she asks him to narrate the Trojans's adventures to date.

Aeneas tells how Troy fell to the Greeks on the night they invaded it by means of a wooden horse. Among other incidents, he describes the murder of Troy's King Priam by the Greek warrior Pyrrhus; the death of his own wife, Creusa; and his own escape with his father, Anchises, his son, Ascanius, and a band of fellow warriors.

On their westward sea voyage, Aeneas continues, the Trojans stopped first at Thrace, where they began to establish a settlement. However, because the ghost of Priam's youngest son, Polydorus, who was killed by Thrace's king, warned Aeneas to flee Thrace, the Trojans left the region and sailed to the island of Delos. There, Aeneas consulted an oracle of Apollo, who told him to seek his ancient homeland, which Anchises understood to be the island of Crete. Unfortunately, when the Trojans reached Crete, they realized that their rightful goal was Italy, so they again set sail. On an island in the Strophadës, they were tormented by Harpies, vicious bird-women, whom they escaped by sailing to Actium and then to Buthrotum.

On Buthrotum, Aeneas and his fellow Trojans were welcomed by its ruler, Priam's son Helenus, and Helenus's wife, Andromachë, the widow of the great Trojan warrior Hector. Helenus advised Aeneas how to reach Italy, and the warriors sailed on to Sicily, where Anchises died at a stopover in Drepanum, whose king, Acestës, received them hospitably. Finally, bringing his story up-to-date and back to the starting point of the narrative, Aeneas describes how the Trojans set forth from Sicily, only to be overcome by the storm that swept them off course.

Dido, inspired with love for Aeneas, confesses her fatal passion to her sister, Anna, who encourages the queen to satisfy it. Juno, hoping to delay Aeneas's arrival in Italy, and Venus, Aeneas's mother, hoping to ensure her son's safety, cooperate to see that Aeneas and Dido are joined in a sexual union, which the queen regards as a marriage. Aware that the Trojan prince is wasting valuable time with Dido, Jupiter, the king of the gods, sends Mercury to instruct Aeneas to sail from Carthage, which Aeneas reluctantly does. Dido, distraught by her lover's departure, puts a curse on the Trojans, the outcome of which will be the Punic Wars, and then commits suicide.

After the Trojans leave Carthage, another storm drives them back to Sicily, where Acestës again gives them a warm welcome. A year has passed since the death of Anchises, in whose honor sacrifices are now made and funeral games are held. Juno, acting through the goddess Iris, incites the Trojan women—tired after seven years of wandering and ready to settle permanently—to burn the ships. Entreated by Aeneas,

Jupiter puts out the fire with rain, saving all but four of the ships. Aeneas, advised by Anchises's ghost, permits any Trojan who wishes to remain in Sicily to do so. Those who want to continue on to Italy are about to sail when Venus, fearing that Juno will again cause trouble, asks the sea god Neptune to guarantee a safe voyage for her son. Neptune does as Venus asks in exchange for one human life, which turns out to be that of Aeneas's ship's pilot, Palinurus, who falls overboard but ably swims to land, only to be slain by savages.

At last, the Trojans reach Italy, known as Latium. Landing at Cumae, Aeneas consults a sibyl and with her visits the underworld. He is welcomed by Anchises's ghost, who describes to him Rome's future and its heroes.

Having seen this vision of Rome's glory, Aeneas begins to establish a settlement in Latium, granted permission to do so by Latium's King Latinus, who is convinced that the Trojans are favored by destiny and so wants to cooperate with them. However, Latinus is frustrated by his subjects, who, under the leadership of the Rutulian prince Turnus, do not trust Aeneas and want to force the Trojans from Latium. Latinus is also besieged by the antagonism of his wife, Amata, who sides with Turnus, to whom she wishes to marry her and Latinus's daughter, Lavinia. Additionally, Latinus is unaware that Juno is plotting the outbreak of war between Aeneas and Turnus.

When war between the Trojans and the Latins becomes inevitable, Aeneas enlists the help of Evander, king of Pallanteum (site of the future Rome), and the Etruscans, who have rebelled against their evil king, Mezentius, Turnus's ally. While Aeneas is out securing this support, the battle between the Trojans and Turnus's forces begins. After Aeneas returns with help from Pallanteum, the war reaches its full fury. Turnus kills Evander's son, Pallas; Aeneas reluctantly slays Lausus, the son of Mezentius; and Mezentius himself is hacked down at the hands of Aeneas.

The Trojans, on their way to victory, assault Laurentum, the citadel of the now-demoralized Latins. Latinus wants peace more than ever, but Turnus stubbornly opposes any type of settlement. After the defeat and death of the warrior maiden Camilla, his ally in battle, Turnus offers to confront Aeneas in single combat, with the understanding that the winner will marry Lavinia and the war cease. After a final attempt by Juno to frustrate the Trojans and Rutulians into breaking the truce, the fight takes place. Aeneas first wounds and then slays Turnus. With this decisive victory, the epic ends.

# List of Characters

## The Human Characters

**Acestës** (uh-**sehs**-teez)   The king of Drepanum, in western Sicily, he gives refuge to Aeneas and his people in Books III and V after storms drive them off course.

**Achaemenidës** (**a**-kuh-**mihn**-ih-deez)   A Greek crewman of Ulysses, he is accidentally abandoned on Sicily, home of the Cyclopes, when his companions flee from the angry one-eyed giants. The Trojans rescue him in Book III.

**Achatës** (uh-**kay**-teez)   Known as "the faithful Achatës," he is Aeneas's armor-bearer and a devoted follower of the Trojan hero throughout the epic poem.

**Aeneas** (uh-**nee**-us)   Romans regarded Aeneas as the ancestor of Augustus—the emperor for whom Virgil wrote the *Aeneid*—and of the entire Roman state, since Romulus and Remus, Rome's legendary cofounders, were believed to be descended from the race of kings established by Silvius, Aeneas's son by his second wife, Lavinia. Aeneas became the object of exceptional veneration by the Romans, the embodiment of all of the virtues that they prized most: steadfastness, courage, patience, obedience to the will of the gods, and reverence for ancestors. As such, he was not only the ancestor of Rome's first emperor but also Augustus's moral prototype, or model, exemplifying in his heroic person all the qualities that loyal Romans attributed to their first emperor.

As a result of this patriotic role assigned to him, Aeneas sometimes appears too good to be true. He possesses a superhuman excellence that makes it hard for us to believe he is a man and not a symbol or a god. Still, Virgil endows him with his share of human qualities: He is subject to discouragement in Book I when his fleet is struck by Aeolus's storm; in Book II, he is uncertain as to what course of action to take on the night that Troy is invaded by the Greeks; and in Book IV, he is torn between his love for Dido and his need to fulfill his mission. Only gradually does he obtain heroic stature, but he is all the more believable because of his initial weaknesses.

**Amata** (uh-**mah**-tuh)    The wife and queen of Latinus, her name—Latin for "beloved"—ironically contradicts the actual nature of this highly disagreeable character. From the moment of her first appearance in Book VII, she is an obstacle to the harmony that Latinus and Aeneas seek. Her influence is always negative: Favoring Turnus rather than Aeneas as the husband for her daughter, Lavinia, she is easily swayed by the fury Allecto, sent by Juno, and becomes a human agent of that goddess's campaign against the Trojans.

**Anchises** (an-**ky**-seez)    As the father of Aeneas by the goddess Venus, Anchises is a venerable figure of wise counsel and instruction, above all in Book VI, when he reveals Rome's future to Aeneas. Aeneas's respect for Anchises exemplifies an important aspect of the Roman virtue *pietas*, the appropriate deference one shows to parents, gods, and country. Virgil strongly implies that the respect paid by Aeneas to Anchises, especially in Book V in the form of funeral games, foreshadows the *pietas* shown by Augustus to his father by adoption, Julius Caesar.

**Andromachë** (an-**drah**-muh-kee)  The widow of the Trojan prince Hector, and later the wife of his brother, the prophet Helenus. She and her husband are visited by Aeneas in Buthrotum in Book III.

**Anna** (**ahn**-nuh)    The warmhearted and impulsive sister of Carthage's Queen Dido, Anna has little importance as a character in her own right, but with her unwise counsel she initiates a series of actions and events that have overwhelmingly important consequences. Good-intentioned, she disastrously encourages Dido to give in to her love for Aeneas and forget her vow to remain chaste and faithful to the memory of her dead husband. Anna's only wish is to see her widowed sister find happiness; ironically, she puts Dido in jeopardy and prepares her to become the victim of two overpowering goddesses, Juno and Venus.

**Ascanius** (as-**kay**-nee-us)    Also known as Iulus; the son of Aeneas and his first wife, Creusa.

**Camilla** (kuh-**mihl**-uh)   A female warrior of the Volscians and Turnus's ally in his battle against Aeneas's forces. In Book XI, she leads a courageous but doomed cavalry attack against the Trojans and their allies. Slain by the Etruscan Arruns, she is avenged by the goddess Diana, who sends the nymph Opis to slay Arruns in turn.

**Creusa** (kray-**ooh**-suh)   Aeneas's first wife, Creusa is a one-dimensional, colorless character, whose sole function is to appear as a sacrificial victim to the great cause of the future Roman Empire by exhorting Aeneas to escape Troy without her.

**Dido** (**dy**-doh)   Unlike most female characters in the *Aeneid*, Dido is a strong woman who possesses heroic dimensions and a will of her own. Leading her people from Tyre after her brother murders her husband, she founds the new city of Carthage, whose construction she is directing when Aeneas arrives there.

Virgil portrays Dido as Aeneas's equal and his feminine counterpart. Her hopeless passion for him is not a flaw in her splendid character: She is forced by Juno and Venus to become his lover, a role that she cannot play for long because fate wills otherwise. Her decision to commit suicide gives her a tragic stature.

**Diomedes** (**dy**-oh-**mee**-deez)   A Greek hero of the Trojan War. In Book XI, he refuses, via a messenger, Turnus's request to fight against the Trojans and their allies.

**Drancës** (**dran**-seez)   A Latin nobleman, in Book XI he acts as an ambassador between Latinus and Aeneas, decrying Turnus's aggressive stance and calling for a peaceful settlement with the Trojans.

**Euryalus** (yu-**ry**-uh-lus)   A young Trojan warrior and the inseparable companion of Nisus, in Book IX, he is slain by the Rutulians while attempting to inform Aeneas of Turnus's attack on the Trojan camp.

**Evander** (ee-**van**-duhr)   Pallanteum's king and Pallas's father, he allies himself with Aeneas, who visits him in his city, built on the site of the future Rome. Related to Aeneas through their common descent from Atlas, Evander is depicted as a benevolent ruler who favors the Trojans's mission.

**Hector** (**hehk**-tuhr)   A son of Troy's King Priam and Queen Hecuba, and the first husband of Andromachë. Hector's ghost appears to Aeneas in Book II on the night Troy is invaded by the Greeks and warns the Trojan prince to flee the stricken city.

**Hecuba** (**heh**-kyoo-buh)   Priam's wife and Troy's queen.

**Helenus** (heh-**lay**-nus)   The ruler of a group of Trojan exiles living in the city of Buthrotum, and Andromachë's second husband. In Book III, he warns Aeneas of the dangers along the sea route to Italy and advises him to consult the sibyl of Cumae.

**Laocoön** (lay-**ah**-koh-uhn)   In Book II, suspecting trickery on the part of the departing Greeks, Laocoön warns his fellow Trojans against bringing an immense wooden horse, left behind by the Trojans's enemy, inside Troy's walls. He and his two sons are slain by two giant sea serpents sent by the goddess Minerva.

**Latinus** (luh-**tee**-nus)   Because the civilization of Rome was supposed to have arisen from the cooperation of the Latin natives with the Trojan newcomers, Virgil found it appropriate to depict the Latin king, Latinus, as a man of moderation and goodwill, ready from the very start to marry his daughter, Lavinia, to Aeneas.

Although Latinus is an admirable character, he is rather ineffectual. He has little place in the action after Book VII, in which he makes his futile bid for peace after having experienced supernatural portents that dispose him in favor of the Trojans. In Book XI, when it appears certain that the Trojans will win, he is again eager to make peace with them, and his terms are generous.

**Lausus** (**law**-sus)   Mezentius's son, killed by Aeneas in Book X.

**Lavinia** (luh-**vihn**-ee-uh)   This sole surviving child of Latinus and Amata is probably the most passive and one-dimensional character in the *Aeneid*, even more so than Creusa, Aeneas's first wife. Destined to become Aeneas's second wife, Lavinia has no will of her own, no personal expression. In Book XI, she is designated as the prize that will be awarded either to Aeneas or to Turnus, depending on who wins their personal battle.

**Mezentius** (muh-**zihn**-tee-us)   The former king of the Etruscans, he was deposed by his own subjects because of his cruelty toward them and becomes Turnus's ally. Virgil portrays him as a complex character: Villain though he is, he is devoted to his son, Lausus, who is slain by Aeneas while defending his father. Mezentius's attempt to avenge his son's death by killing Aeneas endows him with a tragic nobility.

**Nisus** (**ny**-sus)   A Trojan warrior and Euryalus's inseparable companion. In Book IX, he is slain while trying to rescue his friend from Rutulian troops, who waylay the two young Trojans as they are crossing enemy territory with a message for Aeneas.

**Palinurus** (**pa**-lih-**noo**-rus)   Aeneas's steadfast and loyal ship's pilot, whose life Neptune exacts as the price of the Trojans's safe crossing from Sicily to Italy in Book V. Murdered by savages as he swims ashore after Somnus, the god of sleep, induces him to fall overboard, Palinurus, more than any other character in the epic poem, dies as the result of a god's mere caprice.

**Pallas** (**pal**-luhs)   The son of Evander, Pallas resembles Lausus, Mezentius's son, in his youth, bravery, beauty, and *pietas*. Pallas's death at the hands of Turnus in Book X is avenged when Aeneas kills Turnus, who brazenly wears Pallas's swordbelt slung unceremoniously over his shoulder.

**Pandarus** (**pan**-duh-rus)   A courageous Trojan warrior slain by Turnus in Book IX while defending the Trojan encampment.

**Priam** (**pry**-am)   Troy's aged king, who is cut down in his palace by Pyrrhus in Book II during the Greeks's siege of the city.

**Pyrrhus** (**pihr**-rus)   One of the warriors who hide in the wooden horse, he slays Priam's son Politës and then the king himself.

**Sinon** (**see**-non)   The Greek warrior who cleverly persuades the Trojans to bring the wooden horse inside Troy's protective walls.

**Sychaeus** (sy-**kee**-us)   Prince of Tyre and husband of Dido, he is already dead at the time of the *Aeneid*'s action. His spirit is united with Dido's in the underworld, where Aeneas sees them together in Book VI.

**Tarchon (tahr**-kahn)    The leader of Aeneas's Etruscan allies.

**Turnus (toor**-nus)    A prince of the Rutulian tribe and the leader of the Latin forces who oppose the settlement of the Trojans in Latium, Turnus is the only male human character in the *Aeneid* whose stature is comparable to Aeneas's. However, unlike the Trojan hero, who always tries to act for the good of his people, Turnus is motivated by intense pride and a desire for personal fame. His doomed future, sealed by fate, signifies the triumph of the ideal of civic virtue embodied by Aeneas.

## The Gods and Other Nonhuman Characters

**Aeolus** (ee-**oh**-lus)    The god of the winds, who, at Juno's request, unleashes the storm that drives the Trojans off course after they leave Sicily in Book I.

**Allecto** (al-**lehk**-toh)    One of the three furies, female deities who drive their victims mad with rage. In Book VII, Juno uses Allecto's evil influence to incite war between the Trojans and the Latins.

**Apollo** (ah-**pahl**-loh)    The god of prophecy and civilization, he favors the Trojans's mission. Although he appears in person only once in the *Aeneid*, his guiding influence is manifested indirectly through his priests, as in Book III, and through the sibyl of Cumae in Book VI. The emperor Augustus regarded Apollo as his patron and protector.

**Celaeno** (seh-**ly**-noh)    The leader of the Harpies, a band of vicious bird-women, who attack the Trojans in Book III.

**Charon (kay**-run)    The old ferryman who rows the spirits of the dead across the Acheron, one of the underworld's rivers. In Book VI, although Aeneas is a living being, Charon rows him across.

**Cupid (kyoo**-pihd)    The god of love. His mother, Venus, has him inspire Dido with passion for Aeneas in Book I.

**Cymodocea** (ky-**mah**-doh-kee-uh)   The leader of the sea nymphs, formerly the ships of Aeneas's fleet.

**Deiphobë** (day-**ee**-foh-bee)   The sibyl of Cumae. A prophetess and priestess of the god Apollo, she predicts the future for Aeneas and accompanies him on his visit to the underworld in Book VI.

**Diana** (dy-**an**-uh)   The goddess of hunting and protectress of women, especially of virgins like herself. She favors the warrior maiden Camilla, whose death she avenges in Book XI.

**Janus** (**jay**-nus)   A god associated with beginnings, gates, and doorways. In Book VII, Juno throws open the mighty gates of Mars's temple, of which Janus is the guardian, to signify the official beginning of the war between the Trojans and the Latins.

**Juno** (**jyoo**-noh)   The queen of the gods and Jupiter's wife. As the Trojans's most powerful opponent, Juno strives to frustrate and delay the fulfillment of their destined mission to create a new home in Italy. Her hatred, which originates chiefly in events connected with the Trojan War, is aggravated by her knowledge that Rome will surpass her favorite city, Carthage, in world dominance. Only at the very end of the epic, when she is instructed by Jupiter, does she end her opposition to the Trojans.

**Jupiter** (**jyoo**-pih-tuhr)   Also known as Jove, he is the king of the gods and Juno's husband. Although he cannot alter destiny, otherwise he is all-powerful and regulates the actions of all gods. In the *Aeneid*, his role is that of a wise, prophetic father who favors the Trojans.

**Juturna** (juh-**tour**-nuh)   A river nymph of Italian origin, she is the supernatural sister of Turnus, whom she vainly tries to help in Book XII.

**Mercury** (**muhr**-kyoo-ree)   The messenger of the gods. In Book IV, Jupiter sends Mercury to Aeneas in Carthage, to command the Trojan prince to abandon Dido and continue his voyage.

**Minerva** (min-**nuhr**-vuh)   A daughter of Jupiter and the goddess of wisdom, during the Trojan War, she generally favors the Greek cause. In Book II, she lures the Trojans into bringing the wooden horse, which they are told is a Greek offering to her, within Troy's protective walls.

**Neptune** (**nehp**-tyoon)    The god of the sea, who, in Book I, quiets the storm raised by Aeolus. In Book V, he exacts the sacrifice of Aeneas's pilot, Palinurus, as the price of a calm sea during the final stage of the Trojans's voyage to Italy.

**Polyphemus** (**pah**-lih-**fee**-mus)    A Cyclops—a one-eyed giant— who lives as a shepherd on the island of Sicily. In Book III, he and his fellow Cyclopes attack the Trojans when they land near Mount Aetna.

**Venus** (**vee**-nus)    The mother of Aeneas by her mortal lover Anchises, she acts on Aeneas's behalf in opposition to Juno, although she allies herself with the rival goddess in Book IV in an attempt to get her son to settle safely in Carthage as Dido's husband. Eventually, like Juno, Venus resigns herself to the dictates of fate.

**Vulcan** (**vuhl**-kun)    The god of fire and metalworking, whom Venus persuades to forge the arms and protective armor that she presents to Aeneas in Book VIII.

# Character Map

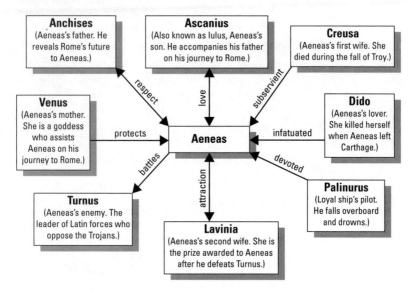

# CRITICAL COMMENTARIES

The sections that follow provide great tools for supplementing your reading of *Aeneid*. First, in order to enhance your understanding of and enjoyment from reading, we provide quick summaries in case you have difficulty when you read the original literary work. Each summary is followed by commentary: literary devices, character analyses, themes, and so on. Keep in mind that the interpretations here are solely those of the author of this study guide and are used to jumpstart your thinking about the work. No single interpretation of a complex work like *Aeneid* is infallible or exhaustive, and you'll likely find that you interpret portions of the work differently from the author of this study guide. Read the original work and determine your own interpretations, referring to these Notes for supplemental meanings only.

# Book I

## Summary

Virgil begins his epic poem with a succinct statement of its theme: He will sing of war and the man—Aeneas—who, driven by fate, sailed from Troy's shores to Italy, where he founded a city called Lavinium, the precursor of Rome. Why, Virgil asks, appealing to the muse of epic poetry, does Juno, the queen of the gods, harass such a good man? He mentions two explicit reasons for Juno's hostility: her love for Carthage and corresponding hatred for the future Rome, which is destined to overthrow her favorite city; and her lingering resentment because Paris, a Trojan, did not award her the golden apple, the prize given to the most beautiful woman in the world. She also hates the Trojans because one of their ancestors was Dardanus, the son of Jupiter—Juno's husband and king of the gods—and Electra, a daughter of Atlas and Juno's rival for Jupiter's affection. Finally, Juno is angry because Jupiter made Ganymede, a Trojan prince, the gods's cupbearer.

Seeing the Trojans set sail for Italy, Juno commands Aeolus, the god of the winds, to raise a storm that will capsize their ships and drown them all. Aeolus obeys her. Many of the ships appear to be lost at sea.

Neptune, the god of the sea, angry because Aeolus has infringed on his own territory, calms the water, and the seven remaining ships of Aeneas's fleet find a safe harbor on the North African coast of Libya, site of the city of Carthage.

Meanwhile, Aeneas's mother, the goddess Venus, reminds Jupiter of his promise that the Trojans will reach Italy and become the forebears of the Roman people. Jupiter quiets her fears by telling her that the Trojans will arrive in Latium; Aeneas will win a great battle and found the city of Lavinium; his son, Ascanius, also known as Iulus, will found Alba Longa, near the future site of Rome; and Romulus will eventually found Rome itself, which will conquer the world, including Greece. Juno will come to love the Romans, and at last a Trojan caesar named Julius, after Aeneas's son Iulus—*not* Julius Caesar, but his heir by adoption, Augustus—will bring an age of peace.

Jupiter now sends Mercury, the messenger god, to Carthage to put the Carthaginians and their queen, Dido, in a mood to receive the

Trojans favorably. The next morning, Aeneas sets out with his companion Achatës to explore the region. They meet Venus, who, disguised as a Carthaginian huntress, tells them that they are near Carthage, a city founded by Dido, who fled with her followers from the Phoenician city of Tyre after her evil brother, Pygmalion, murdered her husband, Sychaeus. Advising Aeneas to go to Dido's palace, Venus assures her son that the missing ships and his comrades are safe. As she turns away, Aeneas recognizes her as his mother and reproaches her for always appearing to him in disguise.

Enveloped now in a cloud that Venus has thrown over them to make them invisible, Aeneas and Achatës observe the people of Carthage at their various tasks. They come at last to a grove, where they find a great temple built to honor Juno. Entering the temple, they see that its walls are covered with decorative panels that depict scenes from the Trojan War, which fill Aeneas with sorrow.

As Aeneas inspects the murals more closely, Dido and her attendants enter the temple. A woman of great beauty and majesty, she seats herself on her throne and holds court. To Aeneas and Achatës's joy and amazement, the men from the missing Trojan ships enter the temple and are received hospitably by the queen, who listens sympathetically as they explain who they are and what has happened to them. At this point, the cloud that shrouds Aeneas and Achatës vanishes, and they are reunited with their companions.

Dido welcomes Aeneas and prepares a banquet in his honor. Aeneas sends for Ascanius, whom Venus, fearing that Juno will again cause trouble, replaces with her own son, Cupid, the god of love, in disguise. She knows that Cupid will fill Dido with passion for Aeneas, thus ensuring the hero's safety. That night at the banquet, Dido unsuspectingly embraces Cupid, thinking that he is Ascanius, and she is filled with love for Aeneas. Overcome by curiosity and admiration, she invites the Trojan hero to describe his wanderings and misfortunes to her and her guests.

# Commentary

Postponing until Book II the account of Troy's invasion by the Greeks, which is the chronological starting point of his poem, Virgil begins the *Aeneid* at what may well be its most crucial and dramatic moment: at the very instant when the Trojans, after many years of wandering, are swept away from their goal of finding a homeland and are stranded on foreign shores that Virgil's readers would have recognized as enemy territory. The elation that the Trojans all felt as they sailed from Sicily is changed to horror and despair, and although by this time Aeneas has been given many prophecies of his eventual success, he must struggle to summon up a brave front for the benefit of his disconsolate companions.

**Literary Device**

This opening book offers an excellent example of the literary device known as in medias res, a Latin expression meaning "in the middle of things." Common to ancient epics, this narrative technique immediately engages readers's attention by getting the story under way at a crucial point in the action. Virgil's beginning Aeneas's story this way allows the events surrounding the fall of Troy and the adventures that ensue to be narrated afterwards by Aeneas himself. Carthage's Queen Dido, already in love with the Trojan warrior, will find many more good reasons to admire him as he unintentionally presents himself to her as a model of heroism.

Throughout the *Aeneid*, the actions of human beings are accompanied by the actions of gods and goddesses, who constantly intervene in human affairs as partisans or enemies, and who are remarkably human in their own passions. Juno, for example, possesses a seemingly inexhaustible supply of grudges against the Trojans. Fittingly, her voice is heard first in the poem, and its tone is outrage: She will be the major impediment to Aeneas's unfortunate struggles to found a homeland. Also dramatically significant is that her appearance as the epic's chief divine antagonist should be followed soon afterward by the entrance of Venus, who, as the hero's indulgent and protective mother, opposes Juno with a force that will ultimately prevail.

In Book I, Virgil seems to pay more attention to divine actions than to human concerns. In addition to our learning about Juno's all-consuming jealousy of Aeneas's fated glory, we see how petty and territorial her fellow gods are. For example, Aeolus is easily bribed to wreak havoc against Aeneas's fleet by Juno's promising him an exquisite nymph for a wife. Juno has obviously favored him in the past: He concedes that he owes her for everything she has done for him. However, like a pair of bickering children, the territorial sea god Neptune chastises his sister Juno and calms his seas.

Although we applaud Venus's protection of her son, she is as manipulative of humans as Juno is. However, because Aeneas is the epic's hero, we are more likely to forgive Venus's indiscretionary power. For example, she causes Dido to fall in love with Aeneas out of fear that the queen otherwise might harm either her son or grandson, or both. However, Venus is not personally against Dido; rather, she is *for* Aeneas. She does not harm Dido as Juno would the Trojan prince.

Detached from the Trojans's distress and the goddesses's passions, Jupiter assures Venus that all is going to be well for her son. He delivers the first major prophecy in the *Aeneid*, a forecast of Rome's national glory. This prophetic vision will be mirrored by the ghost of Anchises, Aeneas's father, when he meets Aeneas in the underworld in Book VI, at the poem's halfway point, and again by Jupiter near the very end of the epic, when the king of the gods tells Juno about Rome's future greatness.

Whereas we typically think of divinities as sources of security and order, Virgil's gods and goddesses—especially Juno—create chaos in an already disordered human world that Aeneas constantly strives to bring to order. Throughout Book I, Virgil emphasizes the continual cause/effect relationship between Aeneas and the deities: Aeolus causes winds to pummel the Trojan ships, and many ships are lost; Neptune causes the winds to dissipate, and Aeneas heads for the nearest shore—which just happens to be near Carthage; and Venus causes Dido to fall instantly and completely in love with Aeneas, who will then languish in Carthage longer than he should.

Against this chaotic backdrop, Aeneas never loses sight of his goal—except temporarily in Carthage—to found a new Trojan state and establish order in his and his countrymen's lives. The theme of order versus disorder is evident in many seemingly unimportant remarks that Virgil makes. For example, when Aeneas anchors his boat off the Carthaginian shore, Virgil writes that he does so "longing for the firm earth underfoot." Aeneas feels more secure on land—a symbol of order—than on sea—a symbol of disorder.

**Theme**

Insignificant tasks assume greater importance than they normally would because they represent the ordered state that Aeneas seeks. When the Trojans land on Libyan shores, one of their first actions is to prepare a meal. Virgil draws noticeable attention to *how* they set about this task: "They skinned the deer, bared ribs and viscera, / Then one lot sliced the flesh and skewered it / On spits, all quivering, while others filled / Bronze cooking pots and tended the beach fires." The Trojans work together, each group of crewmen performing a specified task that, when joined with the other crewmen's tasks, ensures an ordered outcome, even if what is being performed is only the usually mundane cooking of a meal.

Lest we feel that Virgil is more concerned with gods than humans, he provides a well-rounded portrait of his Trojan hero. Almost all of Aeneas's major roles are presented by the end of Book I. His shooting seven stags—one for each of the remaining ships—highlights his role as provider to his people. He is both comforter and motivator when he addresses his companions, rousing their spirits and reminding them that fate has decreed their success. And twice Virgil draws attention to how good a father Aeneas is to Ascanius, describing him as "father Aeneas" and "fond father, as always thoughtful of his son."

The most important role Aeneas assumes is that of dutiful servant of fate and of the gods, entirely faithful to attaining his goal. The epic's opening lines attest to this character trait: Aeneas is "a man apart, devoted to his mission." Later in Book I, Virgil calls him "the dedicated man," and when Aeneas introduces himself to Dido, he describes himself as "duty-bound." Ironically, the more afflicted he is, the greater is his trust in destiny. For example, when he first sees the temple Dido built to honor Juno, "Here for the first time he took heart to hope / For safety, and to trust his destiny more / Even in affliction." No matter how often he feels unfairly treated, he never loses faith in the will of fate.

Had Virgil been satisfied with portraying his hero as the perfect man, afraid of nothing and ideally successful, we would be left with a one-dimensional caricature, a cardboard cutout that was merely an allegorical representation of human virtues. However, Virgil wisely adds human traits and faults to Aeneas's character in order to make him more real, more than just a symbol. For example, when Aeneas, a man capable of human feelings, views the panels in Juno's temple that depict scenes from the Trojan War, the murals bring tears to his eyes as he surveys likenesses of his companions who died in the war. Earlier, when he addressed his distressed countrymen prior to their eating on the shore, he was as "burdened and sick at heart" as his companions. However, his duty as the Trojan leader forbids him to show the insecurity that he feels, which in turn increases his stature as a hero and our favorable opinion of him.

Book I also introduces Dido, one of the poem's three main characters. The portrait that Virgil presents of the Carthaginian queen rivals Aeneas's, although later in the poem our opinion of her will slightly lessen. In Book I, her stature is as noble as her Trojan counterpart, in part due to the similarities between the two. Like Aeneas, Dido fled her homeland under the most trying of circumstances. The story of Dido's personal history, which increases our sympathy for her, rivals the account Aeneas will relate in the following books for its exemplum of noble suffering. Aeneas notes longingly the building of Dido's city, and especially the laws that ensure order in Carthaginian society, an order that he himself so desperately wants for his own people. When we meet the queen, Virgil compares her to the goddess Diana, the great huntress; when Aeneas materializes from the cloud that his mother has shrouded him in, his head and shoulders appear "noble as a god's." And finally, Aeneas notes that Dido is a fair and just ruler of her people, as he himself strives to be. Both characters represent the best of their races. Unfortunately, their relationship is doomed from the start, partly because of Juno and Venus's manipulation of them, and because Aeneas cannot be waylaid indefinitely from his rightful destiny.

Virgil did not invent the episode of Aeneas's visit to Carthage, but it appears likely that the fateful encounter between the hero and Dido, their passionate attachment, and his eventual god-ordained abandonment of her are essentially Virgil's own creation. In an earlier legend recorded by the Greek writer Timaeus, Dido commits suicide rather than marry her suitor, Iarbas, the king whose prayers in Book IV of the *Aeneid* alert Jupiter to Aeneas's overextending his stay in Carthage. According to another legend, which was adopted by Varro, a writer of the first century B.C., it was Dido's sister, Anna, who killed herself for love of Aeneas. Virgil reshapes these stories to provide a tragic and poignant explanation for the enmity that existed between Carthage and Rome.

# Glossary

**buffeted**    beaten back as by repeated blows; thrust about.

**baleful**    harmful or threatening harm or evil; ominous; deadly.

**rankled**    to cause or cause to have long-lasting anger, rancor, resentment, etc.

**mollifies**    makes less intense, severe, or violent.

**founder**    to fill with water, as during a storm, and sink: said of a ship or boat.

**combers**    large waves that roll over or break on a beach, reef, etc.

**portended**    an omen or warning of; foreshadowed; presaged.

**trident**   a three-pronged spear borne as a scepter by the sea god Poseidon, or Neptune.

**incendiary**   willfully stirring up strife, riot, rebellion, etc.

**impend**   [Now rare] to hang or be suspended (*over*).

**fluke**   a pointed part of an anchor, designed to catch in the ground.

**biremes**   galleys of ancient times, having two rows of oars on each side, one under the other.

**poops**   on sailing ships, a poop is a raised deck at the stern, sometimes forming the roof of a cabin.

**auspicious**   of good omen; boding well for the future; favorable; propitious.

**feigned**   [Now rare] fictitious; imagined.

**subjugate**   to bring under control or subjection; conquer.

**circumscribe**   to trace a line around; encircle; encompass.

**cozening**   cheating or deceiving.

**augury**   divination from omens.

**disport**   to indulge in amusement; play; frolic.

**harried**   raided, esp. repeatedly, and ravaged or robbed; pillaged; plundered.

**whelming**   overpowering or crushing; overwhelming.

**acanthus**   any of a genus of thistlelike plants with lobed, often spiny leaves and long spikes of white or colored flowers, found in the Mediterranean region.

**vexed**   troubled, esp. in a petty or nagging way; disturbed, annoyed, irritated, etc.

**blandishments**   flattering or ingratiating acts or remarks meant to persuade.

**stratagems**   any tricks or schemes for achieving some purpose.

# Book II

## Summary

Reluctantly accepting Dido's invitation to tell his story, Aeneas sorrow-fully begins with an account of the fall of Troy. He describes how, in the tenth year of the Trojan War, the Greeks constructed an enormous wooden horse, which they then rumored was intended as an offering to the goddess Minerva in order to gain her protection on their voyage home. In truth, they filled the horse with nine of their best warriors, including Ulysses, and then hid themselves in their ships behind the offshore island of Tenedos.

Fooled by this stratagem, Troy's citizens believed that the Greeks had indeed sailed home. Some wanted to bring the wooden horse into the city; others, rightly suspicious, wanted to destroy it. Laocoön, a priest of Neptune, warned the Trojans that the wooden horse was either full of soldiers or a war machine. Defiantly hurling a spear into the horse's side, he implored his countrymen to remember the last time the Greeks gave a gift to Troy without deception being involved. Of course, the Trojans could not.

At this point, shepherds came to the crowd gathered around the wooden horse. With them was a Greek captive, Sinon, who said that he had deserted Ulysses's army after learning that he was to be sacrificed in order to guarantee a favorable homeward wind for the Greeks. In reality, he was lying: He had been left behind by his fellow Greeks to deceive the Trojans and prepare for the Greek invasion of Troy.

Deliberately confusing the Trojans, Sinon explained that the purpose of the horse was to appease Minerva, who was angry with the Greeks because they had stolen her sacred image, the Palladium, from her temple in Troy; the Greeks had sailed home with the Palladium but would return with it in time and again besiege Troy. Minerva would be pacified only when her sacred image was returned from Greece to Troy with due ceremonial reverence. Sinon then said that if the wooden horse were harmed in any way, the goddess would destroy Troy for its impiety, but if it were brought within the city's walls, Troy would conquer Greece.

The Trojans began to believe Sinon's explanation and were finally convinced of his story's truthfulness after two serpents rose out of the sea and crushed Laocoön and his two sons in their coils, an event that the onlookers regarded as rightful punishment for Laocoön's having attacked the horse. Hoping to make reparation for Laocoön's lack of reverence for Minerva and win the goddess's favor, the Trojans followed Sinon's advice and brought the horse into the city. The real intention of Minerva, who, according to tradition, helped build the wooden horse, was to destroy Troy. She killed Laocoön and his sons because she wanted the Trojans to believe that Sinon's story was true and bring the wooden horse within Troy's walls.

That night, while the weary Trojans slept, Sinon released the Greek warriors hidden inside the horse and opened Troy's gates to the remaining Greek forces, which had sailed back to Troy's shores from Tenedos. The Trojans were helpless against the assault, and Troy was soon in flames. Hector, King Priam's son, who had been slain by Achilles earlier in the Trojan War, appeared to Aeneas in a dream and told him that all was lost, and that he should take Troy's gods of hearth and household—the Penatës—and seek a new city for them.

Waking, Aeneas, disillusioned by the disastrous events revealed in his dream, armed himself and went out into the city, desperately planning to die in combat. He was joined by other Trojans, and after many struggles, including disguising himself as a Greek soldier to more easily traverse the city's streets, he arrived at Priam's besieged palace, where he witnessed the havoc wrought by Pyrrhus, Achilles's ferocious son. Pyrrhus rashly murdered Priam's son, Politës, in front of the king, and then he killed Priam himself at the altar of Jupiter.

Aeneas, suddenly concerned about the fate of his father, Anchises, his wife, Creusa, and his son, Ascanius, all of whom were still at home, began to make his way to them through Troy's streets when he unexpectedly encountered Helen. Convinced that her elopement with Paris was the cause of the war and Troy's downfall, he was seized by a vengeful desire to kill her and would have done so if his mother, Venus, had not appeared and stayed his hand. Venus told him that neither Helen nor Paris was to blame for Troy's destruction; it was willed by the gods, whom she caused to appear to Aeneas in a series of visions that showed them all in a destructive mood.

Aeneas, deciding to flee from Troy with his family, returned home at last, but Anchises, who declared that he would rather die than face exile at his age, refused to abandon his home and urged the others to leave without him, which they would not do despite certain death if they stayed. At that moment, Aeneas and his family witnessed a portent:

A flame appeared around Ascanius's head, and when Anchises prayed to Jupiter for another sign, thunder rumbled—an affirmative omen—and a star streaked across the sky in the direction of Mount Ida. Now convinced that his departure was divinely ordained, Anchises changed his mind; with Aeneas holding his son by the hand and carrying his father on his back, and Creusa following behind, they left the house.

Turning to look for Creusa after the group reached a safe place outside the city that had been designated earlier as the rendezvous point for people wishing to flee Troy, Aeneas discovered that his wife had mysteriously vanished. He went back alone into the chaotic city to try to find her, but, instead, he encountered her ghost, which told him that he was destined to marry again after reaching his new homeland. Returning to Anchises and Ascanius, Aeneas found with them a large number of refugees waiting for him to lead them. As morning came, the band of survivors headed in the direction of Mount Ida.

## Commentary

The destructive invasion of Troy by the Greeks, the subject of Book II, occurs at the chronological beginning of the *Aeneid* and is the first crucial event of the epic, the one from which all others follow in sequential order. Aeneas's personally narrating the Trojans's adventures gives an intimacy to his story that would be lacking if it were told by a third-person narrator. The vivid scenes witnessed by Aeneas, some depicting legendary characters like Helen, Cassandra, Priam, and Pyrrhus, provide great visual impact: We see everything that takes place in the burning city by the light of the flames that are destroying it. Also, Aeneas's recounting these past events enhances our sense of his tale being about a stage in the lives of the hero and his companions that is over and done with, that can only be looked back upon. What lies ahead is the unknown future that awaits the Trojans in their new homeland. The meeting with Dido takes place at a dividing line, a watershed in time, but before Aeneas can sail forth to encounter his future, he must first love and then abandon the Carthaginian queen.

To his description of catastrophic incidents, Virgil adds psychological and spiritual dimensions that give his narrative a particularly human relevance and reveal the compassionate awareness of suffering and the tragic side of life for which he has been justly celebrated. These humane qualities are all the more noteworthy because they are expressed by Aeneas himself, who is thereby presented not only as a man of action but also as a man of feeling, as he was in Book I.

Aeneas is a warrior and a goddess's son, who will lead his people to safety and prepare for the establishment of a new Troy in Italy; but, first of all, he is a human being, at times prone to fear and indecision. Like everybody else in Troy that fateful night the city fell, he went to bed without suspicion, duped like the rest by Sinon and unaware that the city shortly would be in flames. Notably, however, Aeneas is never directly involved in the scenes in which Sinon convinces the Trojans to move the horse within their city's walls. Instead, King Priam himself questions the trickster.

**Character Insight**

Priam's presence at Sinon's inquisition and his actions later in the book show him to be an ineffectual leader of his people. A symbol of all that has gone wrong in Trojan society, he is duped by the lying Sinon, which suggests that he has succumbed to complacency in his rule. Worse, Virgil describes Priam as an "old man" who "uselessly / Put on his shoulders, shaking with old age, / Armor unused for years." Remembering that the Trojan War has been raging for ten years, Virgil's description of Priam's military prowess strongly suggests that the king's physical skills have waned during this time span.

Additionally, our last view of King Priam is not a very flattering one. Hecuba, his wife, questions—perhaps inadvertently, perhaps not—his mental acumen when she asks him what "mad thought" drove him to think he could fight the Greeks. She acknowledges what Priam cannot, that Troy's destruction and his approaching death symbolize the passing of a generation and a way of life. Unfortunately, the new, reigning generation will include individuals like Pyrrhus, who irreverently kills Priam's son in front of the king and then brazenly mocks Priam. When Priam recalls how Pyrrhus's father once nobly showed mercy to the Trojan king, Pyrrhus's response to the memory of his own father is cold, calculated, and inhumanely cruel: "You'll report the news / To Pelidës, my father; don't forget / My sad behavior, the degeneracy / Of Neoptolemus. Now die." In Book III, we learn that even the barbaric Pyrrhus is not invincible; he too becomes a victim of revenge when he is slaughtered by Orestes.

Immediately following this scene, Aeneas remembers his family in their home and worries about their safety. His concern for them, following as it does Pyrrhus's comments about his own father, increases our respect for Aeneas and highlights Pyrrhus's depravity. Lest we fear that Aeneas, as a member of this new generation of leaders, will act as vilely as Pyrrhus, Virgil emphasizes the Trojan hero's independence and honorable character by having him say of himself, "It came to this, That

I stood there alone." This comment recalls Virgil's describing Aeneas in Book I as "a man apart, devoted to his mission."

**Character Insight**

In Book I, Aeneas showed himself to be a competent leader of his people and a responsible father to his son. Here, in Book II, he demonstrates the appropriate *pietas*—devotion to one's family, country, and mission—for his father and again for his son.

When Anchises refuses to vacate his house, nobly choosing instead to commit suicide, Aeneas breaks down in tears and cries out that he could never leave his father. Aeneas is unwilling to abandon him, knowing that Greek warriors could break into the house at any moment and slaughter the man who gave him life. His deep respect for Anchises is best demonstrated by his physically carrying him through Troy's streets to the rendezvous point.

Another admirable role Aeneas continues in this book is that of the good father to Ascanius. Worried for the boy's safety, the Trojan hero's shepherding his son away from danger emphasizes the human nature of his character. After lifting Anchises onto his back, Aeneas recalls how "little Iulus put his hand in mine / And came with shorter steps beside his father." Aeneas's devotion to his son is exemplary.

Aeneas's treatment of Creusa is less admirable than that which he gives his father and son. To a great extent, Creusa's character is one-dimensional, and she appears as a mere prop in this superhuman drama. As the family flees Troy, that she walks behind her husband, son, and father-in-law symbolizes her subordinate position in respect to the males. Aeneas incriminates himself as an uncaring husband when he recalls the events leading up to her disappearance: "Never did I look back / Or think to look for her, lost as she was." His comment, "She alone failed her friends, her child, her husband," seems to place the blame for her death solely on her, when there can be little doubt—especially when she later appears to Aeneas as a ghost—that she was overcome by Greek soldiers and killed.

However, any blame we place on Aeneas for his treatment of Creusa is tempered by the grief he suffers when he learns of her disappearance. His returning alone to Troy when he knows the great danger of his doing so helps redeem him in our eyes. The grief he feels, which Creusa's ghost characterizes as madness, is most evident just prior to his encountering her spirit, when he searches frantically from door to door. Finally, Creusa sanctions his actions concerning her when she asks only that he take good care of their son. Like Jupiter in Book I, Creusa's ghost prophecies

Aeneas's future: She knows the glory that awaits her husband and, even more so, her son, who will become the ancestor of Augustus, to whom Virgil dedicated his epic poem.

Why the Trojans were gullible enough to believe Sinon's story and drag the horse within Troy's walls has been heavily debated by critics. The answer, in part, recalls the theme of order versus disorder from Book I. Throughout Book II, although there is a movement toward a more ordered world for Aeneas and his followers, they are anything *but* safe from their enemy.

The disagreement within the Trojan community about whether or not to drag the horse within the city's walls is an effect of a disordered world in which the Trojans live. Virgil characterizes the discord within the society as "contrary notions" that "pulled the crowd apart." Both the gods and the humans are to blame for this mess that the Trojans—"blind miserable people"—find themselves in: "If the gods's will had not been sinister, / If our own minds had not been crazed, . . . Troy would stand today." Unfortunately, Virgil can only ask these "What if?" questions, for Aeneas now finds himself in search of a new homeland on which to found a new civilization.

The "shadow / Over the city's heart" that the wooden horse casts is both physical and psychological. Physically, the Greek soldiers hiding inside the wooden structure will eventually burn Troy to the ground. Psychologically, the Trojans are "deaf and blind" to the evil they willingly usher into their city, and, as Virgil suggests, their vulnerability is partly due to their living complacently and indulgently: The Greeks make their way unchecked into "the darkened city, buried deep / In sleep and wine." That Aeneas and some fellow Trojan soldiers later disguise themselves in Greek war clothing and are then fired upon by their own men demonstrates just how upside down this world has become.

By the end of Book II, Aeneas has regrouped those of his people who survived the Greek onslaught of Troy. Using a literary device that symbolizes a better future ahead, Virgil writes that a morning star rising over Mount Ida's ridges appears to Aeneas's ragged followers. The Trojan warrior recounts to Dido how he determinedly set forth toward Mount Ida to meet that future: "So I resigned myself, picked up my father, And turned my face toward the mountain range." His resolute attitude is what we—and, more important, Virgil's contemporary readers—expect in this story of a world-class hero.

# Glossary

**twinge**   to cause to have a sudden, brief, darting pain or pang.

**derelict**   neglectful of duty; remiss; negligent.

**gyves**   fetters; shackles.

**chaplets**   wreaths or garlands for the head.

**reparation**   a making of amends; making up for a wrong or injury.

**expiate**   to make amends or reparation for (wrongdoing or guilt); atone for.

**rondure**   a circle or sphere; roundness.

**redoubt**   a breastwork outside or within a fortification.

**conflagrations**   big, destructive fires.

**dominion**   rule or power to rule; sovereign authority; sovereignty.

**clambered**   climbed with effort or clumsily, esp. by using the hands as well as the feet.

**pume**   to foam or froth.

**availed**   was of use, help, worth, or advantage (to), as in accomplishing an end.

**embowered**   enclosed or sheltered in or as in a bower.

**portent**   something that portends an event about to occur, esp. an unfortunate event; omen.

**wraith**   a ghost.

# Book III

## Summary

Continuing his account of how the Trojans came to present-day Libya's shores, Aeneas relates how, at the beginning of the summer following Troy's destruction, the Trojans built a fleet of ships and set forth to seek a new homeland. They landed first in Thrace—now a region in northern Turkey—and were establishing a settlement there when the voice of the dead Polydorus, Priam's youngest son, spoke from deep within the earth and warned Aeneas to flee the kingdom. Priam, who wanted Polydorus out of harm's way during the Trojan War, had entrusted him to the protection of Thrace's king, who had been Troy's ally. The Thracian king, however, had shifted his allegiance to the Greeks during the war and then treacherously killed Polydorus.

After performing funeral rites for Polydorus, the Trojans left blood-stained Thrace and sailed to the island of Delos, sacred to Apollo, from whom Aeneas sought counsel. Apollo declared through his oracle—his priest, through whose mouth he spoke—that the Trojans should seek their "mother of old," which Anchises, Aeneas's father, understood to be Crete, a kingdom ruled by Teucrus, an ancestor of the Trojans.

Following a ritualistic sacrifice to the gods, the Trojans sailed to Crete and attempted to found a city, but their efforts were thwarted by a sudden plague that brought a year of death to humans and crops alike. Anchises then proposed that they return to Delos and again consult the oracle, but this voyage was made unnecessary when Troy's hearth gods told Aeneas in a vision that Apollo's oracle had meant that they should go to Hesperia—Italy—the ancestral home of another ancestor, Dardanus.

On the right track at last, the Trojans again set forth toward Italy, but soon they were driven off course by a storm that forced them to take refuge on one of the Strophadës, a group of islands in the Ionian Sea. Here, Harpies, vicious bird-women, assailed them. The Trojans defended themselves as best they could, and Celaeno, the Harpies's leader, prophesied that after the Trojans reached Italy, famine would drive them to eat their tables as a punishment for their violence against her race.

The Trojans fled from the island and sailed north along the western coast of Greece to Actium, where they spent several months and held athletic contests. From here, they journeyed to Buthrotum, where they were welcomed warmly by the prophet Helenus, a son of Priam, and his wife, Andromachë, the widow of Hector, for whom she still grieved. Helenus warned Aeneas that many trials would still have to be overcome before the voyagers reached Italy, where Aeneas's discovery of a white sow with a litter of thirty young would indicate the site upon which he was to found his city. Telling Aeneas how best to avoid danger while at sea, including the monster Scylla and the whirlpool Charybdis, Helenus also advised him to consult the sibyl of Cumae and to appease Juno's hatred by remembering to offer sacrifices to her.

Andromachë recounted how she and Helenus came to rule together, and provided Aeneas with the information that Pyrrhus, who killed Priam and his son Politës in Book II, was killed by Orestes. Ironically, Pyrrhus's death occurred "before his father's altar," a fitting site for his demise when we remember how cruelly he treated Priam by slaying Politës in front of the Trojan king.

After Aeneas exchanged gifts with his hosts and bid them farewell, the Trojans sailed north to Ceraunia. Here they spent the night and then crossed over to the heel of the Italian peninsula, where Aeneas offered prayers to Pallas and sacrifices to Juno, according to Helenus's instructions. They then sailed across the Gulf of Taranto and, after escaping Scylla and Charybdis, landed on the coast of Sicily, where they spent a fearful night near Mount Aetna, a volcano.

The next morning, the Trojans were accosted by a Greek, Achaemenidës, a member of Ulysses's company, who had been left behind accidentally when his companions fled the Cyclops Polyphemus. He begged the Trojans to take him with them or else kill him, which he said would be a better fate than remaining alone, for not only Polyphemus, whom Ulysses blinded, lived in the region, but many other Cyclopes as well. Polyphemus and other Cyclopes then appeared, and the Trojans fled, taking Achaemenidës with them.

They sailed along the coast of Sicily and finally reached Drepanum, where Anchises, Aeneas's father, died. After burying him, they set sail again and encountered the storm that drove them to Carthage. At this point, Aeneas ends his story.

# Commentary

For the most part, Book III deals with the Trojans's search for their promised homeland, covering almost their entire voyage up to the moment when the storm raised by Aeolus drives them away from their nearby goal of Italy. The ghost of Creusa, whom Aeneas encountered toward the end of the preceding book, had called Italy by its Greek name, Hesperia, but Aeneas does not remember this name during the earlier stages of his voyage, even though it had been entrusted to him under such momentous circumstances. Only after the Trojans's failed attempt to settle on Crete does he fix Italy as his true destination.

While Book III has dramatic moments, it constitutes a relatively placid interlude between two episodes of great intensity—the account of Troy's destruction, with its descriptions of violence and bloodshed, and the tragic story of Dido's passionate love for Aeneas. As such, it resembles Book V, which deals with the stage of the voyage that follows Dido's death and precedes another high point of the *Aeneid*, Aeneas's encounter with the sibyl at Cumae and his descent into the underworld. Books III and V, then, create with the others an overall rhythmical pattern that adds variety of pace to the epic poem's narration.

Although Book III deals with subject matter that may seem more prosaic and uneventful than that of other books, it contributes greatly to the development of the *Aeneid*'s national theme by depicting what Virgil considered unique, important Roman virtues, superimposed on a legendary past. Aeneas's "Roman" qualities are shown especially in his attitude toward Anchises, to whom he constantly gives all his dutiful respect, which the Romans, as members of a patriarchal society, especially valued as an important aspect of *pietas*. Virgil makes a point of telling us that it was Anchises who gave the order to sail from Troy, and that Aeneas consulted his father in Thrace after the hero's ominous encounter with the spirit of the murdered Polydorus, and again on Delos and on Crete. As we shall see, Anchises's authority will be strengthened after his death, for he will be Aeneas's guide in the underworld, and he will predict Rome's future greatness.

Deliberately anachronistic, Virgil also shows how Roman customs and a Roman spirit are already at work in the context of Rome's legendary past. For example, the Trojans perform religious rites in connection with oracular pronouncements and sacrifices to the gods. Repeatedly, Aeneas prays to the gods, both when the Trojans abandon a country and when they arrive at a new one. A notable example of the Trojans's piety is when they take the time to give Polydorus a proper funeral.

Literary Device

The most important divinity in Book III is Apollo. Although he does not appear in person—he reveals himself only once during the entire epic, and then only briefly, in Book IX—he makes his powerful and benign presence felt through every prophecy Aeneas receives. The Penatës, or Trojan hearth gods, who tell Aeneas to sail for Italy, acknowledge Apollo's rule over them; when Aeneas meets Celaeno, the Harpies's leader, she too speaks of how Apollo, the god of prophecy, instructed her to foretell of the Trojan's future; and Helenus, the "Trojan interpreter of the gods's will," receives his gift of revelation from Apollo. The Penatës, Celaeno, and the prophet Helenus strengthen Aeneas's resolve to complete his mission successfully and convince him that a glorious future lies beyond the hardships that he and his followers must endure.

Character Insight

In the course of Book III, we see Aeneas growing into his role as the founder and national hero of a new society. Little by little, the uncertainty that Aeneas revealed in the preceding books gives way to assurance. For example, when the Trojans reach Thrace, Aeneas reports, "I plotted out / On that curved shore the walls of a colony— / Though fate opposed it—and I devised the name / Aeneadae for the people, my own." Later, when Polydorus advises the Trojans to leave Thrace as quickly as possible, Aeneas first consults other leaders of his people: He is a good ruler who does not abuse his power. And before the plague decimates the Trojans and forces their evacuation from Crete, he is well on his way to founding a homeland. The "hoped-for city walls" that he is anxious to erect symbolize the society he so desperately wants to create; his parceling homesteads and decreeing laws are his attempts to bring order and security to his people.

Aeneas's role as a dutiful father is expanded in Book III to include paternal responsibility not only for Ascanius and the Trojans in his immediate care, but for the entire Roman race to come. When Helenus tells Aeneas to "let your progeny / Hold to religious purity thereby," the progeny that the Buthrotum ruler is referring to is that of the Julian line, including Augustus. Helenus's comment is similar to one made earlier by Andromachë, who, concerned for Ascanius's well-being, asks Aeneas if he is fostering "old-time valor and manliness" in his son. These virtues of valor and manliness are prized by Virgil as qualities befitting Aeneas and his Trojan people, and the poet's own fellow Roman citizens.

The Trojans's harboring Achaemenidës, the Greek who is abandoned on the Cyclopes's territory by his Greek shipmates, recalls how the Trojans allowed the trickster Sinon to enter within Troy's walls in

Book II. We wonder just how gullible Aeneas and his people can be to accept so willingly another Greek warrior into their company. Nevertheless, they do. Perhaps Virgil is emphasizing the deep humaneness of the Trojans and, by extension, the poet's own race.

Aeneas's concluding his explanation of how the Trojans came to be in Carthage with the announcement that Anchises, his father, died in Drepanum greatly explains his sorrowful reluctance to recount the Trojans's past when Dido initially asked him to. His dejection over losing his beloved father might also explain why in Book IV he will allow Dido to waylay him from his fate-appointed mission to found a new homeland. Stylistically, note how Virgil parallels the turbulent weather that the Trojans sailed through to reach Drepanum, where Anchises died, to Aeneas's grieving emotions over his father's death: "And in the end the port of Drepanum / Took me in, a landing without joy. / For after storms at sea buffeted me / So often, here, alas, I lost my father, / Solace in affliction and mischance." "O best of fathers," the devoted Aeneas says, and then falls silent, his tale of the Trojans's past having come to an end.

# Glossary

**auguries**   divinations from omens.

**muster**   to assemble or summon (troops, etc.), as for inspection, roll call, or service.

**hummock**   a low, rounded hill; knoll; hillock.

**halyard**   a rope or tackle for raising or lowering a flag, sail, etc.

**filial**   of, suitable to, or due from a son or daughter.

**posterity**   all of a person's descendants.

**caldron**   a violently agitated condition like the boiling contents of a large kettle.

**sanctum**   sacred place.

**roil**   to work hard and continuously; labor.

**welter**   to tumble and toss about, as the sea.

**prophecy**   prediction of the future under the influence of divine guidance; act or practice of a prophet.

**scud**   very low, dark, patchy clouds moving swiftly, generally characteristic of bad weather.

**dallying**   wasting time; loitering.

**whorls**   things with a coiled or spiral appearance.

**infernal** *a*)   of the ancient mythological world of the dead *b*) of hell.

**hawsers**   large ropes used for towing or mooring a ship.

**oracular**   of or like an oracle; wise, prophetic, mysterious, etc.

**auspices**   omens, such as may be revealed in the flight of birds.

**sundered**   broken apart; separated; split.

**immured**   shut up within or as within walls; imprisoned, confined, or secluded.

**cuirass**   a piece of closefitting armor for protecting the breast and back, orig. made of leather.

**caparisoned**   covered with ornamental trappings.

**festal**   of or like a joyous celebration; festive.

**yardarms**   *Naut.* the two halves of a yard supporting a square sail, signal lights, etc.

**boon**   [Archaic] kind, generous, pleasant, etc.

**quail**   to draw back in fear; lose heart or courage; cower.

# Book IV

## Summary

On the morning after the banquet given in honor of Aeneas, Dido confides to Anna, her sister, that the Trojan warrior is the only man she has met since the death of her husband, Sychaeus, who could make her consider breaking her vow to remain faithful to his memory and never remarry. Urging the queen to act on these new, amorous feelings, Anna emphasizes that the dead do not care about the romantic lives of those they leave behind. She advises Dido to pursue the Trojan, both for the sake of her own happiness and for the future safety and prosperity of Carthage, which, Anna says, will be militarily strengthened by the Trojans's remaining presence. Anna's counsel increases Dido's lust for Aeneas, but, unable to act on this passion, the queen languishes helplessly, neglecting her once-paramount project, the half-built new city of Carthage.

Dido and Aeneas's relationship catches the attention of Juno and Venus. For very different reasons—Juno wants to delay Aeneas's reaching Italy, and Venus wants to ensure his safety—the two goddesses jointly conspire to bring about a sexual union of the pair. While Aeneas and Dido are out hunting one day, Juno causes a torrential storm, and the pair seeks shelter in a cave, where they are sexually united. Dido tries to legitimatize the union by calling it a marriage.

News of the relationship spreads throughout Africa. King Iarbas, one of Dido's rejected suitors, vents his anger in a prayer to Jupiter, who sends Mercury to Aeneas to remind the Trojan leader that he is shirking his heaven-appointed duty to found a new homeland: Aeneas must sail from Carthage at once. Shocked into action by Jupiter's command, Aeneas gives secret orders for the ships to be made ready to sail, deciding to postpone notifying Dido of his intention to leave Carthage until the right occasion presents itself.

Dido, however, discovers Aeneas's plan and violently berates him for concealing his intentions from her and for wanting to abandon her to her enemies. Aeneas declares that he did not intend to deceive her, and that he will never forget her, but he does not regard Dido and himself as married, and he must fulfill fate's decrees. His attempt to justify himself only increases Dido's anger. When she sees the preparations for departure going steadily ahead, she loses her pride and sends Anna to Aeneas to beg him to delay sailing until better weather, thus allowing her time to grow accustomed to his leaving. Anna does the queen's bidding, going to Aeneas several times and bringing him to Dido, but Aeneas's resolve to sail to Italy never wavers.

Full of despair and haunted by evil omens and nightmares, Dido secretly decides to kill herself. She asks Anna to prepare a pyre and to heap upon it all the items in the palace associated with Aeneas: These objects, she says, she will burn according to magic rites that will either restore him to her or free her of her love for him. In fact, however, the pyre is intended for burning herself as well as Aeneas's belongings. Ignorantly, Anna does as Dido requests, believing that the queen's grief is no greater than that which she suffered over her husband's death. On top of the newly built pyre, Dido places a couch heaped with Aeneas's clothing, a portrait of him, and his sword, with which she plans to kill herself.

That night, Dido sleeplessly considers her plight. Having ruled out the alternatives of marrying one of her former suitors or following the Trojans, she reaffirms her decision to commit suicide. Meanwhile, Aeneas, asleep aboard his ship and ready to sail the next day, is again visited by Mercury, who appears to him in a dream and commands him to flee while flight is still possible. To strengthen Aeneas's resolve, Mercury deliberately speaks ill of Dido. Aroused, Aeneas gives orders to sail immediately, and soon the Trojan fleet is under way.

When dawn comes and Dido sees the Trojan fleet at sea, she is uncontrollably overcome by an all-consuming rage. She momentarily contemplates having the Trojans pursued; then, realizing that it is too late for this tactic, she curses them, praying that eternal hostility may exist between them and her own people, that some "avenging spirit" will right the wrong that has been done to her, and that Aeneas will "fall in battle before his time and lie / Unburied on the sand."

Resigned now to death, Dido sends her dead husband's old nurse to fetch Anna, pretending to need her sister's assistance in completing magic rites. Once the nurse leaves on this errand, Dido mounts the pyre, lies down on the couch, and stabs herself with Aeneas's sword. Anna arrives amidst the uproar of the household and gathers Dido into her arms, where the queen dies.

# Commentary

Virgil's motive for inventing Aeneas and Dido's doomed love affair is to provide a poetic and romantic explanation for the hatred that existed between Rome and Carthage. The Punic Wars, which occurred between Rome and Carthage in the third and second centuries B.C., would seem to be the fulfillment of the curse Dido places on Aeneas and his posterity when he abandons her and sails to Italy to fulfill his destiny.

**Character Insight**

In addition, Virgil has another important reason for telling this poignant love story: He wants to present Aeneas not only as the embodiment of Roman virtues, but also as a living, breathing human being. We have already seen how Virgil is willing, when the occasion warrants—for example, in his description of the fall of Troy—to show Aeneas as haunted by the same doubts and fears as are other people. Aeneas is not born a hero; he becomes one, and the noble result appears all the more admirable because of the many obstacles he has to overcome.

However, simply to show Aeneas stumbling in the dark would have been a rather negative demonstration of his humanity. Virgil knew that the most effective way to display the hero's humanness would be to portray him in the grips of the strongest of all passions, as a lover whose love is reciprocated. Aeneas's struggle between his love for Dido and his need to prove worthy of his fated mission—which he pursues at the price of sacrificing the personal happiness he craves as much as any man or woman—saves him from becoming a mere one-dimensional character. Later in the *Aeneid*, when he is in danger of appearing to be an unbelievably perfect hero, our recollection that he was capable of loving Dido and reluctantly left her sustains his characterization as a flawed, mortal man.

Had Jupiter not sent Mercury to goad Aeneas into action, it is possible that Aeneas would have remained in Carthage and never would have completed his mission. However, once the Trojan prince realizes his error of remaining too long with Dido, nothing will interfere with his determination to fulfill his destiny: "As the sharp admonition and command / From heaven had shaken him awake, he now / Burned only to be gone, to leave that land / Of the sweet life behind." Facing Dido's wrath once she learns of his pending departure, Aeneas transforms himself from a star-struck lover back to a fate-driven voyager. When he tells Dido that Italy is his only true love, we understand that he has replaced his love for the queen with love for his future homeland. Finally, Virgil's characterizing Aeneas as "duty-bound" recalls this same epithet that the hero used to describe himself in Book I. Although Aeneas is "shaken still" with love for Dido, he returns to his ship and sails to Italy as Jupiter decrees.

Aeneas's responsibilities as a father to Ascanius are called into question in this book, as they were in the previous one. Knowing that the familial relationship between father and son is of great importance to Aeneas—as it is to Virgil—Jupiter questions Aeneas's honor as a progenitor who has seemingly forgotten his son's rightful ancestry. When Mercury, instructed to inform the Trojan warrior in person of Jupiter's concerns, finds Aeneas clothed in Carthaginian finery, the messenger god berates him for failing as a father: "If future history's glories / Do not affect you, if you will not strive / For your own honor, think of Ascanius, / Think of the expectations of your heir, / Iulus, to whom the Italian realm, the land / Of Rome, are due." We know that Mercury's rebuke spurs Aeneas's resolve anew, for later in the book the Trojan prince, speaking to Dido, admits his temporary lapse as a father to "young Ascanius, / My dear boy wronged, defrauded of his kingdom, / Hesperian lands of destiny." He vows never again to forget his responsibilities as a father.

In addition to Aeneas's irresponsible behavior toward his son, his leadership abilities are also dubious in Book IV. His infatuation with Dido affects not only himself but his people, who languish in Carthage. Although Virgil never directly addresses the Trojans's concern for their leader's welfare, he offers clues that indicate the discomfort Aeneas's people feel. When Aeneas informs three Trojan crewmen responsible for readying the fleet to prepare all ships for departure, they gladly obey and eagerly begin stockpiling the vessels. Metaphorically, Virgil compares the Trojans to ants, who work incessantly and without any rest to collect the food that will enable their colony to survive. The image recalls the Carthaginians in Book I, who built their city like bees constructing a hive. Both metaphors emphasize the organization and order needed if a community—such as Rome—is to prosper and run efficiently.

The well-organized society that Dido had created prior to Aeneas's arrival is drastically changed once she becomes infatuated with him. The building of Carthage comes to a complete stop. Even worse, the city's defense against enemy invasion—a concern that Anna uses to urge her sister to pursue Aeneas—is not maintained. In one of the poem's few instances of overtly moral proselytizing, Virgil warns that passion—love out of control—causes disorder, both physically and emotionally, and even affects one impiously: "What good are shrines and vows to maddened lovers? / The inward fire eats the soft marrow away, / And the internal wound bleeds on in silence." Dido affirms that unbridled love fosters chaos when, raging at Aeneas, she scorns the gods. Her faithlessness in the gods and destiny demonstrates just how psychologically mad she has become.

**Character Insight**

Virgil's portrayal of Dido in Book IV is one of the great literary character studies in all of literature. Dido finally knows, as do we, that she is doomed to fail in her conquest of Aeneas, yet we applaud her resourcefulness in facing down her destiny. Her begging at the beginning of Book IV for the earth to swallow her before she falls deeper into passion's indomitable grip is balanced by a similar self-recognition of her plight toward the book's end, when she asks of herself, "What am I saying? Where am I? What madness / Takes me out of myself? Dido, poor soul, / Your evil doing has come home to you." Tragically, no matter how much she is aware of the danger her passion presents, she cannot prevent her own psychological demise.

In some ways, Dido, like Turnus, her male counterpart in the second half of the *Aeneid*, is even more heroic than Aeneas. After all, Aeneas eventually learns that fate is on his side no matter how difficult his journey may be. Dido and Turnus, however, are heroic without this assurance, most of all at the moment of their deaths.

**Style & Language**

Stylistically, Virgil reinforces Dido's inability to control her passion by imagining her as a fire that grows and cannot be quenched. The book's first lines characterize this gnawing, excruciating lust: "The queen, for her part, all that evening ached / With longing that her heart's blood fed, a wound / Or inward fire eating her away." And when Dido discovers Aeneas's intent to leave her city, she becomes "all aflame / With rage." Her burning passion for the Trojan warrior is so great that she becomes physically sick. Fittingly, she dies on a pyre, used for burning corpses in funeral rites. However, her inner flame has been extinguished by her own hand; there is no reason to light the pyre now.

The Carthaginian queen is the plaything, the pawn, of both Juno and Venus. She has no freedom except in her choice to kill herself, an act of courage that proves she is a tragic—as well as a romantic—heroine. Indeed, Dido loses, but the cruel goddesses who use her lose also. In trying against their better judgment to alter the will of fate, they only serve it: The passion that Venus inspires and Juno sanctions is, as fate decrees, frustrated, causing Dido to put a curse on the Trojans, which, in turn, will lead to the Punic Wars.

Although Juno and Venus's intention is to change the fated outcomes of human lives, their manipulative actions are the very instruments of fate that will ensure Rome's triumph and Carthage's defeat. Juno knows that Rome's eventual victory over its rival city has been decreed, but the goddess's attempts to block this outcome ironically make it possible. Likewise, the Romans, although ultimately victorious, will endure hardships—the Punic Wars—that Venus, of whom they are the favored people, does not foresee when she attempts to protect her son by having Dido fall in love with him. Fate moves toward its end as inexorably as water flows down to the sea; it may be forced to change its course a little, but it triumphs over every attempt to prevent its fulfillment.

# Glossary

**quandaries**   perplexing situations or positions; dilemmas.

**wrought**   formed; fashioned.

**erebus**   the underworld.

**dispensation**   the ordering of events under divine authority.

**scruple**   a feeling of hesitancy, doubt, or uneasiness arising from difficulty in deciding what is right, proper, ethical, etc.; qualm or misgiving about something one thinks is wrong.

**copse**   a thicket of small trees or shrubs; coppice.

**contentious**   always ready to argue; quarrelsome.

**retinue**   a body of assistants, followers, or servants attending a person of rank or importance; train of attendants or retainers.

**scabrous**   indecent, shocking, improper, scandalous, etc.

**cowled**   wearing or having a cowl; hooded.

**rills**   little brooks; rivulets.

**spelt**   a primitive species of wheat with grains that do not thresh free of the chaff.

**castigate**   to punish or rebuke severely, esp. by harsh public criticism.

**supplication**   a humble request, prayer, petition, etc.

**ilex**   holly.

**bedew**   to make wet with or as if with drops of dew.

# Book V

## Summary

As the Trojan fleet leaves Carthage behind, Aeneas sees flames lighting the city, and although he is unaware that the fire is from Dido's funeral pyre, he fears for his former lover because he knows that thwarted love has made her desperate. Soon thereafter, an immense storm threatens the ships, and Aeneas follows his pilot Palinurus's advice and sails for Sicily, taking refuge at Drepanum. From there, a year earlier, the Trojans had set out for Italy, only to be swept off course to Carthage. Once again, King Acestës receives them hospitably.

The next morning, Aeneas summons his people and announces that he is going to celebrate funeral rites in memory of his father, Anchises, who died on their previous visit to Drepanum and was buried here. Additionally, Aeneas will hold various athletic games in Anchises's honor. He then makes ceremonial sacrifices at his father's tomb, in the course of which a giant serpent appears. The serpent's puzzling presence seems harmless.

There follows a lengthy description of the athletic games: a hectic rowing contest, in which four ships of the fleet compete strenuously with one another; a foot race, in which Nisus, who falls and loses his own chance of winning, unscrupulously trips another competitor in order to ensure that his beloved friend, Euryalus, will win; a bloody prizefight between two muscular boxers, the Trojan Darës and Entellus, a subject of Acestës; and a display of archery skills made memorable by the flight of an arrow, shot by Acestës, which portentously bursts into flame and disappears from sight. The contests are followed by a cavalry display by the young men, including Ascanius, who will become the forefather of the Romans.

At this point, the happy occasion is spoiled by Juno: She sends the goddess Iris to stir up discontent among the Trojan women, who are tired of traveling and would like to settle permanently in Drepanum. Disguised as one of the women, Iris incites them to set fire to the Trojan ships. Fortunately, Aeneas is notified in time to address prayers for help to Jupiter, who sends a rainstorm that douses the fire, sparing all but four of the ships from destruction.

Aeneas, after wondering if it might be best to forgo his destiny and settle on Sicily, decides to permit the dissenters who want to remain on Sicily to do so. He is encouraged in this plan by Nautës, a Trojan elder, and by Anchises, who appears to him at night in a vision and informs him that shortly they will meet in the underworld after Aeneas has landed in Italy. With the warm approval of Acestës, Sicilian land for a settlement is divided among the Trojans who wish to stay.

After nine days of feasting and sacrificing to honor the site of the new Trojan city, Aeneas and his remaining companions set sail in their refurbished ships for Italy. All appears to be going well, but Venus, concerned as ever for the security of her son and his people, asks Neptune to guarantee a safe journey for the Trojans. Neptune promises to do as Venus asks, but he tells her that one Trojan must be sacrificed in return for the safety of the rest.

That night, Somnus, the god of sleep, causes Palinurus, who keeps watch in the lead ship, to drowse and fall into the sea—he is the sacrifice that Neptune demanded for calm seas. Aeneas, aware that the ship is out of control, takes over the steering, lamenting the loss of his faithful pilot. Book V ends with landfall near.

# Commentary

Book V, like Book III, is less dramatic than those surrounding it. The book that precedes it, which deals with the tragic love of Dido, might be described as a narrative apex whose emotional intensity is enhanced by its being in marked contrast to the generally more placid mood of Books III and V. Book V offers not only a relaxation—in this instance, an easing of tension following the account of Dido's passion and suicide—but a more or less down-to-earth story that heightens, by way of contrast, the otherworldly atmosphere of the book that follows it, in which Aeneas will descend into the land of the dead.

While the emotional pitch of Book V is lower than that of its adjacent episodes, it has moments of excitement and contains downright harrowing incidents. The happy and festive funeral games are followed by the raging fire that, but for Jupiter's intervention, would have destroyed Aeneas's fleet, and by the loss of Aeneas's beloved pilot, Palinurus, who disappears in the sea just before the Trojans reach Italy.

**Style & Language**

Stylistically, Book V's ending is balanced by its beginning, when Virgil introduces Palinurus as Aeneas's able-bodied, pragmatic helmsman. Palinurus's death, which recalls Anchises's at the end of Book III, exemplifies how Virgil interweaves the dark and bright strands of human existence to achieve a subtly balanced and nuanced vision of reality. His commitment to his theme, the glory of Rome, does not blind him to an awareness of the sorrow that accompanies even the most fortunate lives.

While Aeneas by now has been given good reason to believe that his mission is destined to succeed, he is occasionally tried to the point of doubting or forgetting that fate is on his side. For example, after the Trojan women set fire to his fleet of ships, he asks whether or not he should forgo his destiny and make his home on Sicily. Fortunately, he listens to Nautës and his father's ghost, both of whom urge him onward to Italy. That Aeneas respects Nautës's opinion exemplifies what a good ruler he has become. He will hear advice from any who offer it, although the final decision, of course, is his entirely. His parceling land to those Trojans who are tired of traveling and wish to remain on Sicily recalls his similar actions in Book III, after the wanderers reached Crete.

**Character Insight**

Twice in Book V, Aeneas demonstrates his savvy as a leader who knows what speech to give at the appropriate time. After the foot race in which Nisus trips Salius so that Euryalus will win, many spectators balk at Euryalus's proclaiming victory. However, Aeneas decisively settles the matter by declaring Euryalus as the winner. Magnanimously, he gives a gift to Salius and even to Nisus. What is most noticeable is that after Aeneas passes judgment, no one questions his decision: The crowd acquiesces to his ruling. And later, when the boxer Darës loses his match to Entellus, Aeneas shifts the blame for Darës's loss from the boxer's lack of athletic prowess to that which the boxer cannot control: "Don't you feel / A force now more than mortal is against you / And heaven's will has changed? We'll bow to that!" By using the plural "we," Aeneas consoles Darës: If the great Aeneas cannot battle the will of the gods, why does Darës think he can? Aeneas's tactic works well, and Darës is placated.

Another familiar role of Aeneas's, that of the good son, is highlighted by his fulfilling the vow he made to Anchises to celebrate the anniversary of his death. Still deeply respectful of his father, Aeneas's resolve to honor him is noble: "Were I today exiled in Libyan sands / Or caught at sea off Argos, or detained / in walled Mycenae, still I should carry out / My anniversary vows and ceremonies, / Heaping the altars, as I should, with offerings." Aeneas sacrifices to the gods out of respect for Anchises and honors him with celebratory athletic games.

The detailed funeral rites for Anchises would have been familiar to Virgil's contemporary readers. The exemplary piety of Aeneas as he performs the rites is another example of Virgil's infusing the Trojans with virtues that he considered uniquely Roman. He habitually imparts prestige to Roman practices, institutions, and ways of feeling and behaving by tracing their origins to these much-admired people of legend.

Likewise, the athletic games that follow the funeral rites have Roman associations with the Actian games, which Augustus inaugurated in 28 B.C., and which were held every four years thereafter to celebrate the emperor's decisive victory over Antony and Cleopatra in 31 B.C. Augustus was particularly fond of the "lusus Troiae," or "game of Troy," the display of horsemanship with which Virgil concludes the contests in Book V, thus attributing to it a prestigious Trojan origin. As Virgil notes, "Great Rome took up this glory of the founder." This ceremonial equine procession was customarily performed by noble Roman youths, some of whose families claimed descent from the Trojans, among them Ascanius, who was the reputed ancestor of Julius Caesar, the father by adoption of Augustus. Very neatly, Virgil ties all of the genealogical strings together, linking his real Roman present with the legendary Trojan past. His appealing to the past for legitimacy, exceptionally forceful at this point in the Aeneid, anticipates the revelation of Rome's future glory, which awaits Aeneas in the next book.

# Glossary

**profaned**   desecrated, debased, or defiled.

**abeam**   at right angles to a ship's length or keel.

**northing**   *Naut.* the distance due north covered by a vessel traveling on any northerly course.

**interred**   put into a grave or tomb; buried.

**propitious**   that favors or furthers; advantageous.

**affrighted**   [Archaic] frightened; terrified.

# Book VI

## Summary

Saddened by the loss of Palinurus, Aeneas leads his fleet to Cumae, where Deiphobë, the sibyl of Cumae, is led by Achatës to Aeneas while he is visiting a temple built to honor Apollo. She tells Aeneas to sacrifice seven young bulls and seven ewes to Apollo, after which she leads the Trojan prince into a cavern with a hundred mouths that amplify her voice when she delivers Apollo's prophecies. Aeneas prays to Apollo for help in his endeavors to find a new homeland for his people.

Following Aeneas's petition to Apollo, Deiphobë, possessed now by Apollo, predicts much hardship ahead for the Trojans in Italy: They will fight a bloody war, and Juno will continue to oppose them. Aeneas tells the sibyl that he is accustomed to trouble and has already foreseen that many more difficulties lie ahead. Wanting to descend to the underworld in order to visit the spirit of his father, he begs her for help in going there.

The sibyl tells Aeneas that he must find and pluck a golden bough from a tree in an adjacent forest. The bough will allow him to enter the underworld. First, however, he must find and bury the body of a dead comrade. Returning to the beach, Aeneas discovers that the dead man whom the sibyl mentioned is the trumpeter Misenus, who was drowned by the sea god Triton for daring to challenge him in a trumpeting contest.

While hacking pine trees to construct a proper funeral pyre for Misenus, Aeneas sees twin doves, which he instinctively knows were sent by his mother, Venus. The doves lead him to the golden bough, and Aeneas seizes it and takes it to the sibyl's cave. Afterward, he and his companions give their fallen comrade the due rites of cremation and burial.

With these tasks completed, Deiphobë leads Aeneas to the underworld's entrance, a deep cavern at whose threshold sacrifices are made to the gods of darkness. Aeneas and Deiphobë descend through a gloomy region haunted by dreadful spirits and monsters and eventually reach Acheron, one of the underworld's rivers. Here, Aeneas beholds

Charon, the ancient boatman who ferries spirits of the dead across the river, and he observes that the bank on which he stands is suddenly crowded with other spirits, all anxious to cross the river. The sibyl informs him that some of these spirits must wait a hundred years for passage over the river, or until their bodies on earth are buried. Among these, Aeneas encounters Palinurus, who begs to be allowed to cross over with him. Deiphobë chides Palinurus for wanting to break a divine decree, but she also consoles him: In time, a tomb will be built for him, and a cape of land will be named in his honor.

Charon is at first reluctant to ferry Aeneas, a living man, across the river Acheron, but he changes his mind when Deiphobë, commending Aeneas, shows the boatman the golden bough. Disembarking on the other shore, Aeneas and the sibyl find themselves among the wailing souls of dead infants; then, as they proceed, among the spirits of those who were executed for crimes they did not commit; and then among the suicides. They come at last to the Fields of Mourning, the home of those who died of love. Here, Aeneas meets the ghost of Dido. Knowing now that Dido killed herself because he abandoned her, he tries to justify himself to her, saying that he left her unwillingly. Unforgiving, Dido's ghost withdraws from Aeneas and seeks the comforting presence of the spirit of her husband, Sychaeus, with whom she has been reunited.

Aeneas and Deiphobë now come to the fields inhabited by the spirits of men famous in battle, Trojans and Greeks among them. Men who were Aeneas's former companions warmly greet him, but his former enemies fearfully shun him. Among the Trojans he meets is the spirit of Priam's son Deïphobus, who married Helen after the death of Paris, but who was betrayed by her and her first husband, Menelaus, who, with Ulysses, inflicted upon him hideous and fatal wounds that he still bears.

Warned by Deiphobë that time is passing, Aeneas prepares to take his leave of Deïphobus, who describes the two possible paths available to Aeneas and the sibyl. To the left lies the region of Tartarus, a place of eternal punishment for the wicked; to the right lies Elysium, Aeneas's destination. Looking back, Aeneas glimpses Tartarus, the prison of the Titans, whom the gods defeated, and of those who tried to rival Jupiter. Also punished in Tartarus's realm are mortals who have sinned abhorrently, including adulterers, traitors, and incestuous perverts.

At last Aeneas and Deiphobë reach Elysium, which they enter after Aeneas places the golden bough on its threshold as an offering. They

now find themselves in the Blessed Groves, a region of beautiful mead-
ows inhabited by blessed spirits, among them Anchises's. Escorted by
the soul of the poet Musaeus, they find Anchises deep in a lush green
valley, surveying the spirits of his future Roman descendants. After an
exchange of emotional greetings with his father, Aeneas asks about a
river that he sees in the distance and about the souls that hover "as bees"
over it. Anchises tells him that the river is named Lethe, the river of
forgetfulness, and that the spirits filling the air formerly lived on earth
in human bodies; having lost all memory of their former existence after
drinking the water of Lethe, these souls are awaiting their turn to be
born again in new bodies, with new identities that have already been
assigned to them.

When Aeneas asks his father to explain reincarnation to him,
Anchises describes a pageant of historical personalities who would have
been already familiar to Virgil's Roman readers, but who are described
from the vantage point of Aeneas and Anchises in Elysium as belonging
to the future of a city yet to be founded. Among the spirits that Anchises
points out are Silvius, Aeneas's son by Lavinia and the founder of a race
of kings; Romulus, founder of Rome; and the descendants of Aeneas's
son, Ascanius, the Julian family, whose glory will reach its peak with
Augustus, "son of the deified." This "deified" god, Julius Caesar, is also
present. The pageant ends on a note of mourning: Last to be identified
is young Marcellus, Augustus's nephew and heir, who died at the age of
nineteen.

The pageant completed, Anchises leads Aeneas and Deiphobë to the
two gates of sleep, one of which is made of horn, the other of ivory.
Passing through the second gate, Aeneas and the sibyl return to the
world of the living.

# Commentary

Theme

In both theme and placement, Book VI, which many consider to
be Virgil's greatest literary accomplishment, is of central importance
to the development and the ultimate meaning of the *Aeneid*. Here, just
after the Trojans land permanently in Italy, Aeneas descends to the
underworld for his long-anticipated rendezvous with Anchises's ghost,
who reveals Rome's future to his son.

Virgil's imagination and intellect create an otherworldly vision that invites readers to accept it as a symbolic statement concerning the nature of life after death. The possibility of reincarnation, which provides a philosophical basis for the pageant of souls about to be reborn as personages in Roman history, fuses Virgil's speculations on the afterlife with the national theme that lies at the heart of the epic and is its whole reason for being.

The essential philosophical message of Book VI is that the soul, contaminated by its association with the body during mortal life, undergoes purgation after death. Passing on to Elysium, it remains there for a thousand years and is then reborn into the world. The cycles of death, purgation, and rebirth continue until, purified at last, the worthy soul ascends to a state of "fiery energy from a heavenly source." A few exceptionally virtuous souls—like that of Anchises—are free from having to submit to this cyclical process, and they remain in Elysium. Although Virgil does not say so explicitly, presumably they too will ascend eventually to the nebulous Roman spiritual realm.

This cycle of death, purgation, and rebirth is the general interpretation that many commentators have given to the speech Anchises delivers to his son concerning the souls in Elysium. However, because Virgil is dealing with spiritual concepts that by their very nature do not permit a precise, literal expression, no common agreement exists as to these concepts's exact meanings. They can be stated only in terms of symbols and metaphors that stand for a reality that lies beyond ordinary experience. Within this scheme of redemption, the souls of the very wicked, which have gone to Tartarus—hell's equivalent—have no place, being beyond redemption. Of the souls Aeneas encounters elsewhere in the underworld, such as those in the Fields of Mourning, where he meets Dido, nothing is said.

Although Virgil's underworld has an insubstantial, dreamlike quality, it is recognizably a place that is divided into various districts, whose inhabitants are classified according to either the natures of the deaths they suffered or the kinds of lives they lived. Its two most important realms lie in explicitly opposite directions: Tartarus to the left, Elysium to the right. This layout reflects Virgil's concern with abstract concepts and principles, the best illustration of which is the setting of Aeneas's meeting with his father, where almost every detail lends itself to a philosophical or historical interpretation. For example, Aeneas finds his father "deep in the lush green of a valley," an image that emphasizes Anchises's noble and peaceful character while he was alive: In Elysium, he is associated with wisdom and tranquillity because while he lived, he exemplified these traits. Considered as a whole, Virgil's underworld appears to be essentially his own invention, although it contains many traditional details, such as Charon and his ferry; the five rivers—Acheron, Styx, Phlegethon, Cocytus, and Lethe; and the three-headed dog, Cerberus.

The underworld is not only clearly defined; it is also located in an actual region in Italy, in an area to the northwest of Naples where volcanic activity supposedly created an entrance into the underworld. Nearby was the town of Cumae (now Cuma), settled in 750 B.C.—later than the date of Aeneas's purely legendary visit—by Greek colonists from Chalcis, in Euboea. Cumae was the center of a hereditary line of real sibyls—as opposed to the mythical Deiphobë—famous in the ancient world but almost extinct by Virgil's time. As a resident of Naples, Virgil drew upon firsthand impressions of the actual temple of Apollo and the sibyls's cave. These structures, of which only ruins survive, along with the natural surroundings, including Lake Avernus and the woods where Aeneas finds the talismanic golden bough, serve as the basis for Virgil's fictional descriptions of them in Book VI, where everything appears transformed by the light of legend.

Many of the roles previously associated with Aeneas are present in Book VI. Chief among these models of behavior are his exemplary leadership abilities and his deep feelings of humanity. Told by Deiphobë that a Trojan warrior needs burial before Aeneas will be allowed to enter the underworld, the Trojan hero leads his men in offering the proper funeral rites for Misenus. Rather than merely instructing his men on what to do, Aeneas, deeply moved by his Trojan comrade's death, performs the rituals himself: "All who were there / Clamored around the body in lament, / Aeneas, the good captain, most of all." When he meets Dido, who now walks eternally in the Fields of Mourning, Aeneas poignantly weeps. Whether or not he was the primary cause of her demise consumes him: "Was I, was I the cause? / I swear by heaven's stars, by the high gods, / By any certainty below the earth, / I left your land against my will, my queen. / . . . / And I could not believe that I would hurt you / So terribly by going." Tears again come to his eyes when she ignores him and joins the spirit of her first husband. Ironically, although her passion has left her, Virgil characterizes her as a "burning soul," which recalls the many images of fire associated with her in Book IV.

Throughout Book VI, Virgil leaves little doubt that Aeneas's future glory remains fated, no matter how often the Trojan hero questions the outcome of his wandering. For the third time in the poem, he is referred to as "duty bound," and Deiphobë informs him that his troops will reach Lavinian country, named for his wife-to-be. Unfortunately, Lavinia will be one cause of the fighting between Aeneas and Turnus, just as Helen was a cause of the Trojan War. The sibyl also tells Aeneas that he cannot enter the underworld to see his father unless he is able to pluck the golden bough from its tree, which he can do "easily, if you are called by fate." Not surprisingly, Aeneas eagerly breaks the bough effortlessly.

**Literary Device**

Virgil's infusing the Trojans with virtuous qualities that he considered uniquely Roman is evident even in Aeneas's visit to the underworld. When Aeneas meets his former helmsman, Palinurus, the dead pilot attests to his own honorable performance when he describes himself as "duty bound" while trying to steer Aeneas's ship: "I swear / By the rough sea, I feared less for myself / Than for your ship." Clearly, Virgil's Roman readers would have viewed Palinurus's noble attitude as a model attribute of their own civilization. Also, the *pietas* Aeneas has for Anchises while he was alive continues even now that he is dead. Aeneas is most anxious to see his father, and Anchises reciprocates Aeneas's love and respect when he asks his son, "Have you at last come, has that loyalty / Your father counted on conquered the journey?" This notion of *pietas* is best expressed when Virgil, speaking through Anchises's character, says to his fellow citizens, and especially to Augustus, "Roman, remember by your strength to rule / Earth's people—for your arts are to be these: / To pacify, to impose the rule of law, / To spare the conquered, battle down the proud." This statement is one of the few times in the *Aeneid* that Virgil's voice overpowers those of his characters, and his message is clear and concise.

An even more direct address to Augustus is when Virgil, again speaking through Anchises, lauds the ruler's reign. He foretells of the peace and glory this emperor will bring to Rome: "This is the man, this one, / Of whom so often you have heard the promise, / Caesar Augustus, son of the deified, / Who shall bring once again an Age of Gold / To Latium, to the land where Saturn reigned / In early times." Speaking as Aeneas's father to Brutus's two sons, who plotted war against Rome, Virgil warns of the destructive consequences should civil war again break out: "Sons, refrain! You must not blind your hearts / To that enormity of civil war, / Turning against your country's very heart / Her own vigor of manhood." His political agenda is to decry war and glorify his patron's peaceful reign.

Style & Language

Stylistically, Book VI offers some of the most graphic descriptions in all of the *Aeneid*. For example, Deiphobë recounts to Aeneas how Tityos, because of his evil deeds, is unmercifully punished in the underworld by a vulture that "forages forever in his liver, / His vitals rife with agonies. The bird, / Lodged in the chest cavity, tears at his feast, / And tissues growing again get no relief." However, Virgil's intent is not merely to glorify violence. For example, when he writes that Deïphobus's hands are "cruelly torn" and that his nose, "to the noseholes," is "lopped by a shameful stroke," he heightens the great injustice that Deïphobus caused Troy when he was duped by Helen into inaction the night the city fell. The degree of wrong a person does while alive is directly related to the degree of punishment that person's soul receives in the underworld.

## Glossary

**debarked**   unloaded or departed from a ship.

**brutish**   of or like a brute; savage, gross, stupid, sensual, irrational, etc.

**entreaties**   earnest requests; supplications; prayers.

**bestriding**   [Archaic] striding over or across.

**adjutant**   an assistant.

**lament**   to feel deep sorrow or express it as by weeping or wailing; mourn; grieve.

**rowans**   the European mountain ash, a tree with pinnately compound leaves, white flowers, and red berries.

**blazon**   showy display.

**shrouding**   a cloth sometimes used to wrap a corpse for burial; winding sheet.

**bullocks**   young bulls.

**viscera**   the internal organs of the body, esp. of the thorax and abdomen, as the heart, lungs, liver, kidneys, intestines, etc.; specif., in popular usage, the intestines.

**gall**   rude boldness; impudence; audacity.

**hoar**   having white or gray hair because of age.

**thwarts**   rowers's seats extending across a boat.

**bilge**   the rounded, lower exterior part of a ship's hull.

**coracle**   a short, roundish boat made as of animal skins or canvas waterproofed and stretched over a wicker or wooden frame.

**gullets**   throats or necks.

**quailed**   drew back in fear; lost heart or courage; cowered.

**malefactors**   evildoers or criminals.

**jape**   to jest or to play tricks.

**benefactions**   acts of doing good or helping others.

**scourges**   means of inflicting severe punishment, suffering, or vengeance.

# Book VII

## Summary

During the stopover at Cumae, Aeneas's old nurse, Caieta, dies and is buried on a nearby cape that is named in her honor (now Gaeta). The Trojans then sail north, passing the island of the enchantress Circe. At dawn on the following day, they reach the mouth of the Tiber River and dock their ships. At this crucial point of the narrative, the beginning of the second half of the epic, which will deal with the Italian phase of Aeneas's adventures, Virgil again invokes Erato, the muse of poetry, whose help he seeks in order to tell the rest of his story.

Virgil now introduces King Latinus of Latium, who is descended from the god Saturn. Latinus and his wife, Amata, have a daughter, Lavinia, their only surviving child, who is of marriageable age and has many suitors, including Turnus, the leader of the Rutulian tribe. At the exact time that the Trojans arrive at his land, Latinus learns from his deceased father's oracle that he should seek a foreign husband for Lavinia, to be chosen from among strangers who will intermarry with his own people, the Latins, and produce descendants who will conquer the world.

On the shore of the Tiber, meanwhile, the Trojans feast on just-harvested fruits and vegetables; they use hard wheaten cakes as platters on which to heap the food. When they have eaten the food, they then break and eat the wheaten platters: The prophecy that they would settle in the place where hunger forced them to devour their tables has been fulfilled. This prediction, incidentally, was made not by Anchises, to whom Virgil attributes it here, but by the harpy Celaeno in Book III—a discrepancy Virgil would no doubt have corrected had he lived to revise the *Aeneid*.

The next morning, Aeneas sends a hundred gift-bearing men as envoys to Latinus, hoping to win his favor. He then begins laying out plans for his new city. Latinus warmly receives the envoys, for he believes that the Trojans must be the strangers mentioned in the oracle's prophecy. Offering Lavinia as a bride to Aeneas, whom he says he desires to meet, he sends the Trojans back to their leader with gifts of his own.

Learning about this turn of events, Juno is enraged once again. She vows to do her best to forestall the destiny that she realizes must nevertheless be fulfilled: the marriage of Aeneas and Lavinia, and the settlement of the Trojans in Latium. Bent on mischief, she enlists the help of the fury Allecto, whom she commands to foment war between the Trojans and the Latins.

Allecto goes first to Queen Amata, who favors Turnus as her future son-in-law and bitterly opposes her husband's choice of Aeneas, and incites the queen to describe Aeneas to Latinus in the most vicious terms. Amata reminds the king that her choice, Turnus, is also a foreigner, by birth; because his ancestors are Greek, he fulfills the requirement of the oracle. Latinus, however, remains unmoved, enraging Amata to the point that she hides Lavinia.

Next, disguised as an old woman, Allecto visits Turnus and tells him that he must defend his right to marry Lavinia by attacking the Trojans. When Turnus does not take her seriously, thinking that she is merely foolish with age, Allecto then appears to him as the fury she truly is, and he responds by readying his army to fight.

Allecto now flies to the Trojans camped alongside the Tiber River and incites the unsuspecting Ascanius to wound a Latium family's pet stag, thus driving its owners and Latium's populace to retaliate. Hostilities begin, and soon there are casualties. Juno, satisfied by Allecto's mischievous work, dismisses the fury. Latinus's subjects demand battle, but Latinus is opposed to this war against Aeneas's people and withdraws into his palace. Juno immediately takes charge, personally throwing open the twin gates of Mars's temple, a ritual signifying war.

Virgil concludes Book VII with another appeal to the muse for inspiration and with a list of the leaders who, with their warriors, come from all over Latium to fight against the Trojans.

# **Commentary**

The first half of the *Aeneid*, with its great variety of incident, is likely to be more interesting to modern readers than the second half, with its sometimes monotonously lengthy descriptions of battle and bloodshed. However, Virgil expected that his contemporaries would regard the Trojans's campaign in Italy as more significant than the account of Aeneas's wanderings: It deals with nothing less than the establishment of the Trojans in Latium, site of the future Rome, and the ultimate union of the Trojan and Latin races.

The legendary Trojans, as Jupiter assures Juno at the end of the *Aeneid*, will be absorbed into the Latin race that existed before their arrival on Italy's soil. Jupiter's announcement to Juno is intended to reconcile her to the Trojans's presence and make her hospitable toward the future Rome; it is also a way of explaining the total absence of any solid evidence—for example, traces of a language—of the Trojans's real, historical existence.

Aeneas and his fellow warriors are, in fact, Romans in disguise. In the imagined world of the epic poem, they represent all of the virtues admired by Romans, of whom, along with the native Latins, they are supposedly the forebears. Furthermore, they are wreathed with the Homeric glory that derives from their having figured in Homer's *Iliad*, in which Aeneas himself is a hero. Defeated by the Greeks in the Trojan War, the Trojans will be the victors in the war they must now wage in Italy in order to prepare the way for the establishment of Rome, a second Troy.

King Latinus, who recognizes the Trojans's divinely ordained mission from the start, is in favor of Aeneas's marrying his daughter, Lavinia. Virgil carefully creates the impression that the war between the Latins and the Trojans was a mistake that might have been avoided if only the moderate, wise Latinus had prevailed over the wills of Turnus and Amata, who are literally, as a result of Juno's having enlisted the assistance of Allecto, consumed by fury. To his credit, Turnus initially rejects Allecto's counsel, but ultimately he and the queen become the enemies of the civilizing mission represented by Aeneas and endorsed by Latinus.

Virgil leaves little doubt that Aeneas and the Trojans are not to blame for the upcoming, all-out war. On the first full day after his arrival in Latinus's kingdom, Aeneas sends legates bearing gifts to Latinus to ask that the Trojans be allowed peacefully to found a settlement. Always the good ruler, Aeneas begins immediately to outline this hoped-for city. Presented to Latinus, the legates ask only for "A modest settlement of the gods of home, / A strip of coast that will bring harm to no one, / Air and water, open and free to all." Continually, Virgil emphasizes the peaceful nature of the Trojans, who, as Latinus is well aware, are fated to succeed no matter what the obstacles.

**Theme**

Aeneas's outlining where the future city's walls will be erected furthers the theme of order, which is so important in the epic poem. After their chaotic voyaging, the Trojans want nothing more than to settle down quietly. Immediately following the passage describing Aeneas's planning the city, Virgil describes the activities of Latinus's household, activities that symbolize an ordered society, which Aeneas wants for himself and his people. However, when Latinus effectively abdicates his position as king, the Latin society becomes disordered and therefore vulnerable. When Turnus vows to march against Latinus, who has refused to declare war against the Trojans, the king's rule is totally undermined; his own subjects look to Turnus for leadership.

Turnus's militant fury in the second half of the *Aeneid* is the counterpart to Dido's erotic fury in the first half. Together, these two characters are opposed in spirit to the dutiful, self-sacrificing Aeneas, although Turnus and Aeneas are both described as physically superior to other warriors. Splendid individualists who follow their own wills to the point of excess, the Rutulian warrior and the Carthaginian queen embody ways of feeling and acting that prevail in the Homeric epics. The *Aeneid*, however, although it takes much from Homer, is a celebration of the Roman state, to whose future domination Dido and Turnus must be sacrificed.

Book VII, the first book in the second half of the *Aeneid*, resembles Book I in a number of ways: Each has its address to the muse, and in both books Juno foments trouble in order to frustrate Aeneas and the Trojans. Just as Dido welcomed Aeneas, so does Latinus, but the initial harmony in both cases is followed by antagonism: Dido is wounded by Cupid and falls hopelessly in love with Aeneas, and Turnus, aroused by Allecto, overrides Latinus's peaceful intentions.

**Character Insight**

Similarities between other characters from the first half of the poem and those in Book VII abound. Perhaps the greatest is that of King Priam, Troy's ruler, and King Latinus. Physically, both are old and feeble: In Book II, Virgil describes Priam as "the old man . . . shaking with old age"; at the time the Trojans arrive in his land, Latinus has "now grown old." In terms of their effectiveness as rulers, both kings are unable to stop an onslaught of their peoples. Priam finds refuge in his wife's arms, and Latinus shuts himself away in his palace, dismissing all responsibility for running his kingdom.

**Literary Device**

Additionally, once Dido and Amata are infected by overwhelming desire—Dido in her lust for Aeneas, and Amata to see her daughter marry Turnus—both vent their frustration similarly. Virgil says of the Carthaginian queen: "Unlucky Dido, burning, in her madness / Roamed through all the city." Of Amata, he writes: ". . . the poor queen, now enflamed / By prodigies of hell, went wild indeed / And with insane abandon roamed the city." Not only is the image of fire linked to both women, but each roams her respective city in a state of psychological madness.

**Literary Device**

The spirit of the *Iliad*, which appears in many places throughout the second half of the *Aeneid*, is most evident in Book VII, in the list of the warriors summoned by Turnus to fight against the Trojans. Roman readers would have likened Virgil's cataloging to that of Greek and Trojan warriors in Book II of Homer's epic. In the *Aeneid*, the listing of warriors and their lineage underscores the importance Virgil placed on *pietas*, or patriotism and duty. He first introduces a combatant and then includes the man's noble ancestry. For example, he describes the twin brothers Catillus and Coras as "progeny / Of Argos, by descent from Amphiaraus." Of special note are Mezentius and his son, Lausus, both of whom will appear again in Book X. In all, Virgil's cataloging demonstrates the deep respect he and his contemporaries had for familial relationships, the foundation for a successful society.

# Glossary

**colloquies** conversations; esp., formal discussions.

**repose** to rest or lie at rest.

**legates** governors of a Roman province, or their deputies.

**striplings** grown boys; youths passing into manhood.

**overture** an introductory proposal or offer; indication of willingness to negotiate.

**diadem** an ornamental cloth headband worn as a crown.

**requisite** required, as by circumstances; necessary for some purpose; indispensable.

**snood** a baglike net worn at the back of a woman's head to hold the hair.

**surfeited** indulged or supplied to satiety or excess.

**temerity** foolish or rash boldness; foolhardiness; recklessness.

**thong** a narrow strip of leather, etc., used as a lace, strap, etc.

**subverted** overthrown or destroyed.

**railed** spoken bitterly or reproachfully; complained violently.

**cudgel**   a short, thick stick or club.

**shindy**   a noisy disturbance; commotion; row.

**interposed**   introduced (a remark, opinion, etc.) into a conversation, debate, etc.; put in as an interruption.

**kine**   cows; cattle.

# Book VIII

## Summary

As armies march from all over Latium to fight the Trojans, Turnus extends his appeal for help to Diomedes, who had engaged Aeneas in personal combat during the Trojan War and is now a ruler in southern Italy. Aware of this dangerous course of events, Aeneas anxiously tries to devise a plan of action.

One night while Aeneas is sleeping, the god of the Tiber River appears in a dream and tells the Trojan prince that he will find on the shore a white sow and her litter, which symbolically represent Alba Longa, to be founded by Ascanius after thirty years have passed—the number of sucklings in the litter. This discovery is the sign Helenus foretold to Aeneas: It is absolute proof that the Trojans have come to the right place at last. The river god also advises Aeneas to sail upstream to the city of Pallanteum and seek the aid of its king, Evander.

Waking, Aeneas prays to the river god and then finds the sow and her litter, all of which he sacrifices to Juno. He then sails up the Tiber with two of his oared ships and their crews. The next day, approaching Pallanteum, they come upon Evander, his son, Pallas, and a crowd of citizens, who are engaged in worshipping Hercules.

Aeneas, identifying his own people and his mission, is warmly received by Evander, a Greek who came to Italy with his people many years before and established Pallanteum, on the site of the future Rome. Aeneas tells Evander that the two are blood relatives: Dardanus, the founder of Troy and Aeneas's ancestor, was the son of Electra, Atlas's daughter; Evander's father, Mercury, was the son of Maia, another of Atlas's daughters.

Evander, who recollects having met Priam and Anchises when he was a young man, promises his full support against Turnus. He invites Aeneas and his company to be guests at the worship ceremony for Hercules, which is performed yearly as an offering of thanks to Hercules for killing Cacus, the fire-breathing giant who dwelt in a nearby cave and victimized Evander's people.

Aeneas accompanies Evander to his home, and on the way Evander tells Aeneas that the region of Latium was formerly the realm of the god Saturn, who, banished by Jupiter, came here as an exile and taught the arts of civilization to the savage natives. In Pallanteum, Aeneas is shown sites that will be famous in later times when Rome is in its full glory, including the Capitol, the future city's central hill.

That night, Venus visits her husband, Vulcan, the blacksmith of the gods, and persuades him to make weapons and armor for her son. The next day, Vulcan goes to his shop and orders his three smiths, who are Cyclopes, to begin the work. In Pallanteum, meanwhile, Evander advises Aeneas to go to the nearby city of Agylla—or Caere, now Cerveteri— a stronghold of the Etruscans, to seek their help. Having overthrown their evil king, Mezentius, who now has taken refuge with the Latins, the Etruscans are prepared to wage war against their former ruler. Because a seer has told the Etruscans that they must choose a non-Italian to lead them, they will welcome Aeneas as their leader.

Aeneas, at first doubtful about asking the Etruscans for help against the Latins, is given a go-ahead by his mother—tremendous crashes of thunder—and soon sets off for Agylla with Pallas, four hundred horsemen, and the pick of his own crew, the rest of whom he sends back to the Trojan camp downstream with a message to Ascanius informing him of what has happened.

At Agylla, Aeneas's company joins the Etruscans, who are under the leadership of Tarchon. Here, Venus appears before her son with the arms and armor that Vulcan has forged for him. The masterpiece of the ensemble is a magnificent shield decorated with episodes from Roman history, of which Aeneas, of course, can have no knowledge, since all of these events lie in the future. The shield's center depicts the crucial naval battle at Actium, which will mark the defeat of Antony and Cleopatra and the triumphant return to Rome of its future emperor and Virgil's patron, Augustus.

# Commentary

Book VIII, in which Aeneas consolidates his position by gaining the support of Evander and the Etruscans, offers a tranquil interlude between the irreversible steps leading up to war, detailed in the preceding book, and the outbreak of hostilities depicted in Book IX. Because we first view Evander as he is performing rites for Hercules and other gods, our impression of him is favorable; he embodies deep, sincere religious piety comparable to Aeneas. Likewise, we favor the Etruscans when we learn that they have deposed their evil king, Mezentius, who resembles Turnus in his savage arrogance and unbridled fury. Like the Trojans, Evander and his people are foreigners in Italy, and their presence is also opposed by Turnus. Furthermore, Evander is related to Aeneas through their common descent from Atlas.

**Theme**

Aeneas's visit to Pallanteum affords Virgil the opportunity to link the city of his own present, Rome, to its legendary predecessor. In the course of Aeneas's city tour, the Trojan prince views urban sites that were familiar to Virgil's contemporary Roman readers. This patriotic history lesson was intended to demonstrate the continuity of Roman institutions and to impress readers with the idea that as long ago as the heroic age, the time in which the *Aeneid* and Homer's epics are set, destiny had already selected the spot on which Rome would rise, as well as ordained the greatness of the Romans themselves.

**Literary Device**

Book VIII is saturated with references that link the legendary past to the Rome of Augustus. Virgil uses every means put at his disposal by legend and myth to show the Augustan Age as having been especially favored by fate and the gods. And, once again, Virgil's political purpose—to legitimize Augustus by showing him as the heir of the ages—is enhanced by allusions to Homer's *Iliad*.

This continuity of past and present is dramatically emphasized at the very moment that Aeneas and his band approach Pallanteum: They encounter Evander and his people performing rites of thanksgiving to Hercules at the same altar—the *Ara Maxima*, or "the Greatest" altar—where annual rites in honor of Hercules were still being performed in Virgil's own time. Virgil counted on his informed readers to be aware of this conjunction and to make a comparison between Hercules, Pallanteum's savior, and Augustus, who became Rome's savior by defeating its enemies and thus ushering in an age of peace.

**Character Insight**

Throughout Book VIII, Virgil draws parallels between Hercules, Aeneas, and Augustus as past, present, and future heroes—relative to the time of the story. In the past, Hercules killed Cacus; in the present, Aeneas is about to conquer Turnus; and in the future, as revealed on the shield that Venus presents to her son, Augustus will defeat the combined armies of Antony and Cleopatra. Later, in the course of the ceremony honoring Hercules, the dancing priests—the Salii—sing honorific hymns for the Greek warrior, a ritual detail that would have reminded Virgil's readers of the deep respect paid to Augustus after Actium, the site of his victory over Antony and Cleopatra, when members of the same ancient priesthood inserted his name into their hymns.

Comparisons between Aeneas and Hercules are also implied in the hymn sung by the dancing priests, who recount how Hercules performed many labors and was opposed by Juno—or Hera, her Greek name— who was his great enemy before she became Aeneas's. The many labors undertaken by Hercules in myths about him parallel the endless tasks Aeneas performs to establish a homeland. Numerous details in Book VIII stress the likeness between the two heroes, as when Aeneas performs rites for Hercules and then sets out for the Etruscans's camp on a horse covered with a lion's skin, an emblem associated with the Greek hero.

Although Virgil presents Turnus only once in Book VIII, at its beginning when the warrior "raised the flag of war," this lone view is enough to cement our dislike of the Rutulian. Turnus is linked with disorder, and because of his rash behavior, "Then hearts were stirred by fear, then all of Latium / Joined in distracted tumult, and young men / Grew bloody-minded, wild." In comparison, Aeneas is thoughtful and concerned about the senseless bloodshed he knows is imminent. The passage in which Virgil describes the Trojan hero as "heartsick at the woe of war" directly follows Turnus's spurring others to madness and increases Aeneas's noble stature when compared to his adversary's all-consuming passion for war.

# Glossary

**weltered**   tumbled and tossed about, as the sea.

**biremes**   galleys of ancient times, having two rows of oars on each side, one under the other.

**suppliant**   asking humbly; supplicating; entreating.

**grotto**   a cavelike summerhouse or shrine.

**aegis**   a shield borne by Zeus and, later, by his daughter Athena and occasionally by Apollo.

**blandishment**   a flattering or ingratiating act or remark, etc., meant to persuade.

**slothful**   indolent; lazy.

**cuirass**   a piece of closefitting armor for protecting the breast and back, orig. made of leather.

**sistrum**   a metal rattle or noisemaker consisting of a handle and a frame fitted with loosely held rods, jingled by the ancient Egyptians in the worship of Isis.

# Book IX

## Summary

Eager to get the war under way, Juno sends Iris, a lesser goddess, to inform Turnus that he must take advantage of the absence of Aeneas, who has gone to win the support of Evander and the Etruscans, by attacking the Trojans now. Immediately responsive, the Rutulian warrior marches against his enemy. Rather than risk combat in the open, the Trojans withdraw into their camp to guard the ramparts, as Aeneas advised them to do before he left for Pallanteum.

Unable to reach the protected Trojans, Turnus decides to burn their ships. However, before the ships can be set ablaze, Jupiter, in answer to a plea from his mother, changes them all into sea nymphs, who swim away unharmed. In acting as he does, Jupiter fulfills a promise he made to his mother years before, when Aeneas built the ships from pine trees taken from her grove on Mount Ida, near Troy, where the Trojans found refuge after their defeat.

Turnus is not disturbed by the fleet's transformation. In fact, he regards the ships's disappearance as favorable: The Trojans now have no means of escape. Because night is coming, he delays another attack until the next day and orders his forces to rest until then.

In the Trojans's camp, the inseparable companions, Nisus and Euryalus, who appeared in Book V as contestants in the foot race, volunteer and obtain permission to go to Aeneas in Pallanteum in order to inform him of the siege; hoping together to perform a glorious act of bravery, they are fearless. They go with the approval of their elders and Ascanius, who promises them that both he and his father will richly reward them.

Nisus and Euryalus pass safely through the enemy's encampment, killing many warriors who lie in a drunken sleep. However, on the road to Pallanteum, they are intercepted by the Rutulian captain Volcens, who is leading a force of three hundred men to Turnus's aid. The young Trojan men flee into a forest, where they become separated. Nisus manages to shake off pursuit and leave the woods, but Euryalus, who is hampered by armor he took as spoils from the Rutulian camp, is captured. Nisus, who has already reentered the forest to look for his companion, discovers him in enemy hands and boldly launches spears, killing two warriors. To avenge these deaths, Volcens slays Euryalus, provoking Nisus to slay the Rutulian captain in turn, only to die himself of wounds inflicted by Volcens's defenders.

Volcens's men proceed to Turnus's encampment, where the carnage inflicted by Nisus and Euryalus causes great consternation. The next day, the two Trojans's heads, impaled on spears, are exhibited to the Trojan defenders at their ramparts, and the battle begins. A great struggle follows, with Turnus's forces attempting to scale the Trojan camp's walls, only to be beaten back. A tower crashes, causing many deaths; two survivors are slain, one of them, trying vainly to get back over the wall, by Turnus. Ascanius, who slays Remulus, Turnus's brother-in-law, with an arrow to punish him for mocking the Trojans's manhood, is visited by Apollo, who praises the young Trojan prince for his skill but tells him that henceforth he must refrain from killing, as his purpose will be to promote peace.

Now, to provoke the Latin enemy, the brothers Pandarus and Bitias, guardians of the Trojan gate, fling it open. Latin warriors force themselves through it but are beaten back, while Trojans leave the camp and fight outside. Turnus slays Bitias, and the Latins, aroused by Mars, increase their assault as Pandarus manages to close the gate, shutting out many Trojans. Turnus, however, slips into the camp before the gate is shut, and a struggle ensues between him and Pandarus. The Rutulian prince, aided by Juno, is the victor. He proceeds to cause havoc among the Trojans, but they gradually get the upper hand. Undaunted by the vast number of Trojans fighting against him, at the very moment of greatest danger, Turnus escapes death by leaping fully armed into the Tiber River and swimming back to join his fellow warriors.

# Commentary

In Book IX, with Aeneas away in Pallanteum, the Trojans and the Latins engage in indecisive warfare, and the situation at the end resembles what it was at the start. The battle, which continues over a period of two days, shares our attention with the intervening nighttime tragedy of Nisus and Euryalus.

Virgil contrasts the serenity of Aeneas in Book VIII with the frenzy of Turnus in Book IX. The Trojan leader has been assured, first by his tour of Pallanteum and then by the scenes depicted on the shield presented to him by his mother, of eventual victory over Turnus's forces. In a way, Rome already exists in the form of Evander's city, and the course of its triumphant history has already been laid down. Although Juno would like Turnus to believe that he has a chance of claiming victory over the Trojans, in actuality, the reader, gods and goddesses, and Aeneas all know that Turnus is bound to be defeated by the Trojans, and that his strenuous efforts in this book and those that follow must all come to nothing.

Book IX is the only book in the *Aeneid* in which Aeneas is absent. However, his spirit and his inviolate leadership still govern the warriors under his command. When Turnus's army first attacks the Trojan encampment, the Trojans pull back within the security of their walls, as Aeneas instructed them to do before he left to seek allies. Virgil notes that the retreating soldiers's impulse is to fight, but they respect Aeneas's leadership and withdraw as he had commanded them to do.

Aeneas's presence is also felt through his son's actions. Knowing that his father's duties as leader include rousing the troops, Ascanius assumes this responsibility when he promises gifts to Nisus and Euryalus before they depart on their ill-fated mission. His address to the two boy-soldiers recalls Aeneas's speech made to the athletic competitors in Book V, in which he promised gifts to the participants. Ascanius also reminds us of his father when, having killed one of the enemy for the first time, he refrains from boasting of his accomplishment. Because a good ruler does not needlessly inflame his enemies, Ascanius limits himself to a very short speech. Virgil's brief comment following Ascanius's speech emphasizes the brevity of the boast: "Only this / Ascanius called out." As Virgil noted earlier in the book, Aeneas's son is "thoughtful, responsible / Beyond his years"; Ascanius will make as good a leader as his father.

With Aeneas out of the picture, Turnus, who manages to enter the Trojans's camp and make his desperate bid to defeat the newcomers to Italy, stands forth as Aeneas's antagonist—his chief enemy and heroic counterpart. Concerning Turnus's character, critical opinion has always been divided. However, it seems fairly obvious that since Turnus's role in the epic is to embody the forces that will be defeated by fate's decree, he is condemned to behave in a way that must necessarily portray him as the inferior of Aeneas, whom fate favors.

We read of Turnus's rage in this book with the certain knowledge that he is fighting a lost cause, even though he believes that he has a chance of winning. This ironic knowledge is likely to dispose us to feel rather sorry for him in spite of his faults, as Virgil, who was never content to give a one-dimensional picture of human nature, perhaps intended.

Turnus's actions hinge on his rash personality. Described from the book's outset as "the rash prince," this character flaw proves to be his undoing. For example, after gaining entrance into the Trojans's camp, he begins slaughtering his enemies with reckless abandon, consumed by his thirst for blood. However, his lack of control hinders rather than helps his cause. Instead of admitting his own troops within the enemy's walls, he fights alone and thus misses the chance to claim a decisive victory, as Virgil notes explicitly: "And if the thought had come to the champion / To break the gate-bars, to admit his friends, / That would have been the last day of the war, / The last for Trojans. But high rage and mindless / Lust for slaughter drove the passionate man / Against his enemies." Earlier associated with the fire imagery of Dido's uncontrolled passion for Aeneas, Turnus's lust for blood thwarts what should be his overriding concern, to defeat the Trojans as quickly as possible and thereby marry Lavinia.

Book IX is the most graphically violent book in the *Aeneid*. However, the violence is not indiscriminate; rather, it emphasizes the depravity of Turnus's character. Although Turnus is not personally responsible for Nisus's and Euryalus's deaths, his parading their severed heads, skewered on spears, shatters completely our sense of dignity to which the dead have a right. The great injustice of Turnus's performance is reinforced by Euryalus's mother's heartfelt wailing over the loss of her son. Her reaction increases the beastliness of the Rutulian's actions. Although Turnus has the power to make the "quivering" earth resound, as he does when he slays Pandarus, his ghastly behavior is in marked contrast to the noble character of Aeneas, whose stature gains even in his absence.

The two central characters of the intervening episode, Nisus and Euryalus, are familiar to us from Book V, in which Nisus, who fell as he was about to win a foot race, tripped another contestant to ensure that his inseparable companion, Euryalus, would win instead. Now, Nisus, surrendering his own favorable situation, tries ineffectually on a far graver occasion to save his friend's life and dies. Nisus and Euryalus are in the ranks of a number of young people in the *Aeneid*—Pallas, the son of Evander; Lausus, the son of Mezentius; and the warrior maiden Camilla—who, as beautiful as they are brave, must die in battle. The pathos surrounding their deaths heightens our sense of the cruelty of war, even a war that is fought, like the present one, for what is held to be a good purpose.

# Glossary

**inscribing**   writing, marking, or engraving (words, symbols, etc.) on some surface.

**lustral**   of, used in, or connected with ceremonial purification.

**rampart**   an embankment of earth, usually surmounted by a parapet, encircling a castle, fort, etc., for defense against attack.

**conflagration**   a big, destructive fire.

**marauders**   raiders who rove in search of plunder.

**visage**   the face, with reference to the form and proportions of the features or to the expression; countenance.

**carrion**   the decaying flesh of a dead body, esp. when regarded as food for scavenging animals.

**gittern**   an early instrument of the guitar family, having an oval body and wire strings.

**poltroons**   thorough cowards.

# Book X

## Summary

Jupiter, summoning the gods, instructs them about the policy they are to follow in dealing with the humans's on-going war. Overruling both Venus and Juno, who argue in favor of the Trojans and the Latins, respectively, he declares that there is to be no further divine intervention. The war's outcome must be left to fate.

Meanwhile, the fighting outside the Trojans's camp grows more furious, and there are many casualties on both sides. With a fleet of thirty ships filled with Etruscan warriors and Evander's forces, Aeneas begins the journey from Agylla to where the battle is being fought. During the night, before the fleet finally lands near the battle scene, the sea nymphs who were previously Aeneas's ships approach the fleet. Their leader, Cymodocea, tells Aeneas about the siege of his troops that is now taking place.

When the Trojans see Aeneas arrive in his magnificent armor, they take heart. Turnus and the other enemy leaders do not panic, however, but launch an attack on Aeneas and his forces almost as soon as they land. A great slaughter follows, and Aeneas does his share of the killing. Pallas, proving his own courage, rallies his men when their spirits wane. He leads them in attacking the forces of Lausus, Mezentius's son, whom he engages in a battle of equals: Both are young, brave, and handsome. Also, both are fated to die: first, Pallas at the hands of Turnus, who spears him and takes his richly illustrated swordbelt as a trophy; and then Lausus, whom Aeneas will slay. Foreseeing these deaths, Hercules grieves, but Jupiter consoles him by stating that all men must die, but in dying they can win the fame that comes from performing valorous deeds.

Enraged by the news of Pallas's death, Aeneas slashes and kills his way through the enemy ranks in search of Turnus. Jupiter, waiving his rule against intervention, allows Juno to save Turnus by creating a shadow-Aeneas as a diversion. Turnus mistakes the fake Aeneas for the real man and pursues him on board a ship, which Juno then floats off to sea, preventing the Rutulian prince from risking his life in combat against his Trojan counterpart.

As Turnus rages with frustration aboard the ship, Aeneas, after a vain search for him, vents his bloodlust on the Etruscans's former king, Mezentius, whom he wounds in the groin. Unable to continue fighting, Mezentius drags himself to safety while Lausus takes up the fight. Aeneas warns Lausus not to fight him, but when Lausus scoffs at this advice, Aeneas effortlessly kills him, only to be moved to pity by Lausus's death and the young man's selfless love for his father.

Mezentius, who receives Lausus's body from his son's comrades, is overcome by grief and remorse. Although he is gravely wounded and knows that he will probably be slain, he mounts his horse and rides off to fight Aeneas. He is determined to avenge Lausus's death, which has made his own life meaningless, and to atone for his evil deeds. Mezentius fights bravely, but Aeneas finally kills him after felling his horse, which pins him to the ground. Before receiving the fatal stroke, Mezentius begs Aeneas to see that his body is buried in the same grave as his son's.

## Commentary

In Book X, with both protagonist and antagonist present for the first time, the war enters its crucial phase. Turnus's killing Pallas will lead eventually to his own death, for Turnus arouses in Aeneas a lust for vengeance that transforms the Trojan leader into an unrelenting enemy. Aeneas's fury will be heightened by the sight of Pallas's swordbelt, which Turnus unceremoniously wears as a war trophy during his battle with Aeneas in Book XII. There, the Trojan hero will dismiss from his mind the fleeting thought of sparing Turnus and will lead him instead to give the final, killing thrust that brings an end to both Turnus's life and the epic poem.

Literary
Device

Book X concludes with Aeneas slaying his other great antagonist, Mezentius. This incident is one of the most powerful in the *Aeneid* and offers an outstanding example of Virgil's ability to introduce, at the very moment of triumph for the victor, a note of pathos that opens us to sympathy for the victim. Virgil's power to awaken this feeling is all the more remarkable because in this case the victim, Mezentius, is monstrous. Although gravely wounded, Mezentius takes on a heroic stature by fighting Aeneas to avenge his son's death and make amends for his own evil past.

In his grief over Lausus, whom Aeneas reluctantly slays, Mezentius resembles Evander, who loses Pallas. The love that exists between fathers and sons—Aeneas and Anchises offer the greatest example—is perhaps the most powerful emotional tie portrayed in the *Aeneid* and is closely bound up with the ideal of *pietas*—patriotism and duty.

Mezentius also contrasts—negatively—with Aeneas, at least in terms of their respect for the gods. Addressing the Trojan leader before flinging his spear at him, the evil king deliberately calls on no god to steady his aim, claiming that his right arm is the only god he needs. Aeneas, however, described as "the God-fearing captain" whose aim is true, successfully wounds his enemy. The man who is submissive to the gods wins in battle; the heathen does not.

In addition to religion, fate affects the outcomes of many battles here in Book X. Nowhere is this better exemplified than when Jupiter, speaking to Hercules, who wishes to help Pallas fight Turnus, philosophically explains death's unstoppable march: "Every man's last day is fixed. / Lifetimes are brief, and not to be regained, / For all mankind. But by their deeds to make / Their fame last: that is labor for the brave." However, despite a person's fated death, Jupiter does allow for some leeway, at least concerning Turnus. When Juno petitions her husband to permit Turnus to live a short while longer, he grants her wish. He tells her that there is room for some lenience concerning when a man must die, but she deludes herself if she thinks Turnus will be spared forever from his fate.

While modern readers tend to find the first half of the *Aeneid* more engrossing than the second, Virgil himself regarded the second half as fulfilling the true purpose of the epic and expected his readers to feel the same. We, however, may sometimes find his descriptions of man-to-man combat wearisome, especially in Book X, in which these military contests go on longer than elsewhere. Still, Virgil's readers probably appreciated the elaborate descriptions of carnage. We must remember that the Romans were a warlike people: They relished gladiatorial fights, and persistent warfare was the means by which Rome forged its empire. Furthermore, war was regarded as the noblest theme of epic poetry.

Virgil especially emphasizes a warrior's code of honor against which combatants are judged. Generally, those warriors who respect the unspoken code will prosper, but those who flaunt their victories will die. Such disparity concerning honorable actions is nowhere greater than between Turnus and Aeneas.

**Character Insight**

Turnus is the anti-hero, the character who, because of his ignoble behavior, is fated to die. His wish that Pallas's father, Evander, were present to witness his son's death recalls Pyrrhus's horrific killing of Politës, witnessed by the young soldier's father, Priam. Once Turnus kills Pallas, he boasts of his accomplishment; worse, he defames the sanctity of death when he steps on Pallas's dead body and then dishonorably removes the fallen man's swordbelt. Of these actions, Virgil comments, "The minds of men are ignorant of fate / And of their future lot, unskilled to keep / Due measure when some triumph sets them high. / For Turnus there will come a time / When he would give the world to see again / An untouched Pallas, and will hate this day, / Hate that belt taken." Turnus is a poor winner who will pay—with his life—for his insolent behavior.

Aeneas, on the other hand, greatly respects a warrior's code of conduct. Faced with Pallas's death, his actions underscore his humaneness, for death is not trivial to him as it is to Turnus. Remembering the time he spent with Pallas and Evander, Aeneas offers sacrifices in the young soldier's name. Later in the book, he again exhibits noble qualities when he mourns the death of Lausus, an enemy. Visibly moved by this death, Aeneas "groaned in profound pity. He held out / His hand as filial piety, mirrored here, / Wrung in his heart." Of all the characters in the poem, Aeneas knows best the "empty rage" and "painful toil" of war.

It is in Book X, which focuses almost entirely on the war between the Trojans and the Latins, that Virgil most closely embraces Homer's *Iliad* as a model for his own epic poem. For example, the council of the gods recalls the beginning of the *Iliad*'s Book VIII, in which Zeus convenes his fellow gods and orders them not to interfere in the war between the Greeks and the Trojans. More important, apart from this and other specific references to Homer's epic, Virgil echoes the overall tone of the *Iliad*'s battle scenes. Like Homer, he succeeds in convincing us of his characters's humanity. They remain accessible to feelings of love and sympathy even in the midst of struggle and death.

# Glossary

**subjugating**   bringing under control or subjection; conquering.

**terebinth**   a small European tree of the cashew family, whose cut bark yields a turpentine.

**presage**   a sign or warning of a future event; omen; portent.

**shingle**   large, coarse, waterworn gravel, as found on a beach.

**emulating**   trying, often by imitating or copying, to equal or surpass.

**scion**   a shoot or bud of a plant, esp. one for planting or grafting.

**bemused**   muddled, stupefied, or preoccupied.

**tableau**   a striking, dramatic scene or picture.

**carnage**   bloody and extensive slaughter, esp. in battle; massacre; bloodshed.

**bastion**   any fortified place; strong defense or bulwark.

**integuments**   natural outer coverings of the body or of a plant, including skin, shell, hide, husk, or rind.

**rout**   an overwhelming defeat.

**enchased**   engraved or carved with designs, etc.

**spectral**   of, having the nature of, or like a specter; phantom; ghostly.

**pillory**   any exposure to public scorn, etc.

# Book XI

## Summary

At dawn the next day, Aeneas, sick of slaughter, hangs Mezentius's armor on a big oak trunk as a memorial to the fallen king and as a sign of victory, and then tells his men that the time has come to march on Latinus. But first, he says, the dead must be ceremonially burned and buried, and Pallas must be returned to Pallanteum. Aeneas mourns for the slain youth and pities his father, Evander, who is unaware of his son's death. Pallas's body is placed on a bier and sent off with an escort of a thousand men, plus spoils of war, sacrificial captives, and Pallas's horse, riderless. This procession is followed by a line of mourners.

Now envoys come from Laurentum seeking a truce and asking Aeneas to allow the return of the Latin dead for burial. Aeneas grants this request, saying that he wants peace, and that he is willing to engage Turnus in single combat as a way of resolving the conflict. The Latin envoy Drancës, who is a bitter enemy of Turnus, praises Aeneas and expresses the hope that Aeneas and Latinus will become allies. During the truce, which lasts for twelve days, the Trojans and the Latins live together peacefully and honor their respective dead.

At Pallanteum, Evander and his people receive Pallas's body. The king laments that he himself did not die instead of his son, but he declares that he does not blame the Trojans for his son's death, and that he is consoled by the thought that it was for a good cause—to help the Trojans establish themselves in Latium. Evander sends back the men in the escort with a message for Aeneas: The Trojan leader owes him Turnus's death.

On the battlefield, Aeneas and Tarchon, the Etruscans's leader, oversee the funeral rites for their dead, which include the sacrifice of animals, the burning of the dead soldiers's bodies, and the burial of the ashes. The Latins do the same, and fires burn for three days. Meanwhile, there is great mourning in Laurentum and much opposition to the war and to Turnus's proposed marriage to Lavinia. Drancës insists that Turnus should fight alone against Aeneas in order to settle the issue since Turnus is the one who most opposes the Trojans's settling in Italy. However, Queen Amata defends Turnus against such criticism.

Increasing the Latins's despair, messengers now arrive from the southern Italian city of Arpi with a message from its king, Diomedes, to whom the Latins have appealed for aid, announcing that he has refused their request. Nothing but evil, Diomedes declares, has happened to those who fought against the Trojans during the Trojan War. He enumerates the mishaps that have befallen him: His companions were changed into birds, he lost his wife, and he was exiled from Argos to his present kingdom as punishment for having wounded Venus. Furthermore, having engaged in personal combat against Aeneas, he is all too familiar with the Trojan's physical prowess.

Discouraged, Latinus declares that the war against the Trojans is hopeless, and that they should be welcomed to Latium and given land or, should they choose to go elsewhere, given ships. He proposes to send envoys with gifts to them. Drancës approves and, motivated by jealousy of Turnus, says that Lavinia should wed Aeneas. Repeating his earlier proposal, he says that if Turnus objects to these arrangements, he should face Aeneas in single combat. In reply, the indomitable Turnus declares that victory over the Trojans is still possible; although Diomedes has declined to fight, there are others who will help, including the famous Volscian woman warrior, Camilla. If no additional forces come to aid the Latins, Turnus says, then he will fight hand to hand against Aeneas and settle the issue.

In the midst of this quarreling, a messenger arrives with the news that the Trojans and Etruscans are marching on Laurentum. Turnus responds by calling his forces to arms. Amata, Lavinia, and a throng of women go off to pray to Athena.

Turnus and Camilla together prepare for Laurentum's defense: Turnus leads his forces into a forest, where he intends to ambush the main body of Aeneas's army, while Camilla and her cavalry of men and women engage the enemy's cavalry. Despite great bravery, Camilla is slain, and her forces flee into Laurentum. When Turnus receives the news of Camilla's defeat, he abandons his ambush and hastens with his own army to the city, only to encounter Aeneas's forces, which have already arrived at the gates unopposed. Night falls before a battle can occur, and both armies camp outside Laurentum.

# Commentary

Style &
Language

Book XI is an interlude between the battle described in the preceding book, which brings the Trojans close to victory, and Aeneas's defeat of Turnus in direct combat, which concludes the war and the epic poem. Structurally, the present book falls roughly into three parts: the first section describes the truce and the return of Pallas's body to Evander in Pallanteum; the second section deals with the Latins's council of war, held to determine what course of action to take against their enemy; and the final part is devoted to the brave but hopeless battle waged against the Trojans and their Etruscan allies by the forces of the warrior maiden Camilla, who is believed to be entirely Virgil's creation, although she and her female compatriots recall the Amazons, mythical women warriors. Book XI is stylistically unified by the sun's rising in the first line and its setting in the last few lines as the armies prepare to battle.

Theme

Aeneas's model behavior as a brave warrior tempered with compassion continues to be a major theme. The Trojan prince prepares the proper funeral rites for the dead and discharges his "ritual vows / As victor to the gods." He is in marked contrast to Turnus, whom we never observe making ritualistic offerings for his fallen comrades.

Character
Insight

As Aeneas readies Pallas's body for transport back to Evander, his weeping over the death of this newfound and now-lost friend and ally reminds us of this god-like hero's human frailty. However, good Trojan commander that he is, Aeneas's emotions do not overwhelm his sense of duty. Virgil's staccato lines mimic Aeneas's fierce determination to end the war: "That was all. / Then he turned backward toward the parapets / And made his way to camp." Aeneas's resiliency is again demonstrated later in the book when the Latins, arguing amongst themselves, debate their will to continue the war. Their disordered behavior is juxtaposed to Aeneas's ordered behavior, which Virgil characterizes in the succinct line, "Meanwhile Aeneas left camp / And took the field." Desiring peace for himself and his people, Aeneas will fight only if he has to, but his actions assure us that he is ready to do battle if that is what his future holds.

Theme

The glory of dying honorably in battle, which Virgil and his fellow Romans esteemed, receives much attention in Book XI. For example, when Evander meets the procession that carries his dead son, he is stricken with grief over his loss, but his emotions are tempered by his remembering the great deeds that Pallas accomplished in fighting side by side with Aeneas. By winning "the beauty of courageous death," combatants assure their place in history because their exploits will not be forgotten. This immortality is best expressed by Opis, who, sent by the goddess Diana to watch over Camilla, promises the warrior maiden that her death is not in vain: "Yet your queen has left you / Not without honor at the hour of death, / Nor will your end be unrenowned / Among earth's people, nor will it be known / As unavenged." As the *Aeneid*'s own cataloguing of ancestral lines attests, dying with honor is valued not only because it reflects the combatant's virtuous character, but because a family's reputation is often at stake.

# Glossary

**parapets**   walls or banks used to screen troops from frontal enemy fire, sometimes placed along the top of a rampart.

**interment**   the act of interring; burial.

**bier**   a platform or portable framework on which a coffin or corpse is placed.

**heady**   impetuous; rash; willful.

**cortege**   a ceremonial funeral procession.

**palpable**   clear to the mind; obvious; evident; plain.

**legates**   governors of Roman provinces, or their deputies.

**inviolable**   not to be violated; not to be profaned or injured; sacred.

**derided**   laughed at in contempt or scorn; made fun of; ridiculed.

**appease**   to pacify or quiet, esp. by giving in to the demands of.

**pre-empted**   seized before anyone else can, excluding others; appropriated beforehand.

**curvets**   in equestrian exhibitions, a movement in which a horse rears, then leaps forward, raising the hind legs just before the forelegs come down.

**guile**   slyness and cunning in dealing with others; craftiness.

**impiously**   not piously; specif., in a manner lacking reverence, respect, or dutifulness.

# Book XII

## Summary

With the combined Trojan and Etruscan forces at Laurentum's gates, Turnus becomes fully aware that the Latins are in grave danger, so he renews the offer he made earlier in the citadel before Latinus and Drancës: He will fight Aeneas alone, and the winner will have Lavinia for his wife.

Both Latinus and Amata try to dissuade Turnus from this resolution, which they recognize as foolhardy, but Turnus stubbornly sticks to his decision and sends his herald to inform Aeneas that both sides are to join in a truce, and that he and Aeneas will fight the next day at dawn. That night, Turnus inspects his horses and his armor, whetting his appetite for battle, while Aeneas, equally aroused, rejoices in the armor that Vulcan made for him at his mother's request.

At dawn, the two armies meet on a plain near the city. Juno, however, fearful for Turnus, summons Turnus's sister, the river nymph Juturna, and bids her to go to her brother's aid, either to save him from death or to break the truce. On the plain, sacred rites are performed, and Aeneas vows to the gods that if Turnus wins the fight, the Trojans will withdraw to Pallanteum and no descendants will ever attack the Latins in the future. He promises that if he should win, he will claim nothing for himself: The Latins and the Trojans will live together peacefully as equals; he will marry Lavinia; and her father, Latinus, will retain his power. Latinus solemnly agrees to these terms and declares that from this time on there will be peace.

The Rutulians, however, are discontented. Juturna, moving among them disguised as one of their nobles, takes advantage of the Rutulians's restless mood: Because they outnumber their opponents two to one, she declares, they should be ashamed to let one man do the fighting for all of them. Angered, the Rutulians are ready to break the truce. At this moment, a pack of waterfowl dive and threaten an eagle that has seized a swan; when the eagle releases the swan, the Rutulians take this act as a portent signifying that they, too, will be victorious if they resist Aeneas.

They are encouraged by an augur, a priest adept at reading bird omens, who hurls his spear at the Trojans and thus initiates a resumption of hostilities.

Aeneas, who vainly attempts to restore the broken peace, is wounded by an arrow and forced to leave the field. His withdrawal raises Turnus's fighting spirit to the point that Turnus goes mad with bloodlust and kills as many opponents as he can reach. Meanwhile, Venus heals Aeneas with a magic herb: The enemy arrow drops from his wound, and his strength is miraculously restored.

Returning to the field, Aeneas rallies his forces and goes in pursuit of Turnus. Juturna, meanwhile, who has cleverly taken control of her brother's chariot by disguising herself as its driver, drives Turnus all over the field, keeping him safe from an attack by Aeneas, who goes wild with frustration and, like Turnus, kills without stint. Venus now directs her son's attention to the fact that Laurentum's citadel has been left undefended by the Latins, whereupon Aeneas commands his men to attack it immediately, to the horror of the citadel's Latin inhabitants. Fearing that all is lost and that Turnus is dead, Amata hangs herself in despair.

On the battlefield, Turnus hears cries coming from the besieged citadel and tells Juturna that he has finally seen through her disguise as his charioteer. At this point, a warrior coming in haste from Laurentum informs Turnus about what has been happening in the city and announces the queen's death. He mockingly points out that Turnus, the famous warrior, has been driving over an empty meadow—a fact to which Turnus now fully awakens, filled with remorse. Turnus tells Juturna that now he will fight Aeneas alone, as he promised earlier.

Turnus and Aeneas meet outside Laurentum, and the long-awaited battle takes place. Full of confidence, the Rutulian strikes the Trojan with his sword, which is not his own powerful weapon but one belonging to his original chariot driver, taken by mistake. The sword shatters immediately upon contact with Aeneas's armor. Calling on his men to bring him his proper sword, Turnus withdraws as Aeneas pursues him. The Trojan prince hurls his spear at the Rutulian prince, but the spear gets immovably lodged in the trunk of a sacred olive tree in answer to Turnus's prayer to the god Faunus. Juturna brings her brother his true sword, but Venus intervenes and enables Aeneas to extricate his spear.

The duel continues, watched by Jupiter and Juno from a golden cloud. Jupiter tells Juno that Aeneas is about to win and that she can do nothing more to hinder him. Juno promises to cease her opposition to the Trojans, but she asks her husband to permit the Latins to retain both their language and their name. Jupiter grants these requests and tells Juno that out of this alliance of Latins and Trojans will come an indomitable race—the epic's final prophecy, which matches the one Jupiter made to Venus in Book I.

Jupiter now sends a fury to earth disguised as an owl, which darts at Turnus and fills him with terror. Juturna withdraws in discouragement, realizing her helplessness in the face of such an omen. Aeneas advances at Turnus with his spear as the Rutulian, making a last, desperate effort, heaves an enormous rock at Aeneas. The rock falls short, and Turnus, paralyzed by fear, is knocked down by Aeneas's spear, which strikes him in the thigh. Helpless, Turnus says he is resigned to dying, but he begs Aeneas to see that his body is returned to his father. Moved by this plea, Aeneas considers sparing Turnus's life, but then he sees that the dying warrior is wearing Pallas's swordbelt as a trophy. This reminder that Turnus killed Aeneas's dear friend arouses the Trojan hero's anger, and he remorselessly thrusts his sword into Turnus's chest, killing him.

## Commentary

**Literary Device**

The tragic, somber, final line of the *Aeneid* and the epic poem's ringing, declamatory opening line signify the two emotional poles of the epic. Their positioning has a symbolic as well as a narrative importance, for between the moods to which they give voice, the poem constantly moves back and forth as it unfolds. The establishment of Rome is achieved only through the human suffering of Aeneas and his people, and of his opponents—Dido in the first half of the epic, and now, at the end, Turnus.

Virgil's vision of reality was too honest to allow him to see life other than as a mixture of good and evil elements. Had Virgil been merely a propagandist for Augustus, he might easily have finished the epic on a triumphant note. For example, he could have concluded it with the conversation between Jupiter and Juno in this final book, with the king of the gods assuring his consort of a glorious future for the Romans, whose protector she would happily become.

Instead, Virgil gives the epic's final line to the last moment in Turnus's life, the moment that marks the utter, hopeless defeat of a man who is stripped of his glory and virility and becomes a moaning ghost. Aeneas's victory is complete, but it must be paid for by the downfall of a worthy enemy, for whom nothing remains but a retreat into the shadows of the underworld.

The epic's final lines, "And with a groan for that indignity / His spirit fled into the gloom below," are the same that, in the preceding book, described Camilla's death. The repetition reinforces the likeness between Camilla and Turnus, friends and allies in a battle for a lost cause, both cut down in the prime of their youth.

**Character Insight**

Turnus's fate, however, unlike Camilla's, is mitigated by his inability to control his emotional rage. This lack of control reaches its height in Book XII, which we expect since the book details the final conflict between Turnus and Aeneas. The rage Turnus felt at the end of Book XI carries over to the beginning of Book XII, in which his passion is described as "hot and unquenchable." Virgil, as he did earlier with Dido, associates Turnus's intense feelings with fire. The uncontrollable lust that consumes the Carthaginian queen is similar to Turnus's overwhelming craving for Lavinia: "Desire stung the young man as he gazed, / Rapt, at the girl. He burned yet more for battle." The greater Turnus's passion for Lavinia, the greater his wanting to do battle, yet his military judgment is clouded by his passion for the young princess. As Virgil notes of Turnus toward the poem's end, "He did not know himself. His knees gave way, / His blood ran cold and froze."

Surprisingly, Turnus redeems himself—at least partly—when he finally accepts that it is not his fate to win against Aeneas. We sympathize with Turnus's plight, especially when, speaking resignedly to his sister, he acknowledges the ignoble afterlife that awaits him. His speech to her is notable for its timeless questioning of what death holds for all of us: "To die—is that / So miserable?" Ultimately, Turnus's greatest fear is not dying; his greatest concerns are the opinions that others will have of him after he is dead and, as with all of the other warriors in the poem, how his reputation will affect his family's good name.

Aeneas, who wants nothing more than to end the war, rouses himself to battle as passionately as his antagonist does, but Aeneas's reasons for wanting to do battle are radically different from Turnus's. Aeneas understands that by fighting Turnus one on one, only he or the Rutulian will die, and not the many warriors who would were the all-out war to continue. Even when large-scale battle again breaks out, Aeneas does not kill any of his enemies; instead, he seeks Turnus exclusively, knowing that if the renegade warrior is killed, then his followers will cease fighting. As Aeneas tells Latinus, he wants no kingdom for himself. His only goal, as it has been throughout the entire epic, is to build a city in which he and his displaced countrymen can settle peacefully.

The fight that finally ensues between Aeneas and Turnus is described as earth-shattering. After all, the fate of the civilized world hangs in the balance. Virgil emphasizes the universal importance of the battle when he writes that the earth groaned from the crashing of the warriors's shields. Even more cataclysmic is the groan "heard echoing on all sides from all / The mountain range, and echoed by the forests" when the Rutulians realize their leader has fallen. The epic poem has been leading up to this grand finale, and every detail here at its end furthers the sheer magnificence of the founding of Western civilization's greatest empire.

# Glossary

**maw** the throat, gullet, jaws, or oral cavity of a voracious animal.

**myrrh** a fragrant, bitter-tasting gum resin exuded from any of several plants of Arabia and East Africa, used in making incense, perfume, etc.

**inviolate** not violated; kept sacred or unbroken.

**despoiled** deprived of something of value by or as by force; robbed; plundered.

**careering** moving at full speed; rushing wildly.

**lave** to wash or bathe.

**firebrands** pieces of burning wood.

**vying**   that vies; that competes.

**profaned**   treated with irreverence or contempt; desecrated.

**pestilence**   anything, as a doctrine, regarded as harmful or dangerous.

**immedicable**   that cannot be healed; incurable.

# CHARACTER ANALYSES

The following character analyses delve into the physical, emotional, and psychological traits of the literary work's major characters so that you might better understand what motivates these characters. The writer of this study guide provides this scholarship as an educational tool by which you may compare your own interpretations of the characters. Before reading the character analyses that follow, consider first writing your own short essays on the characters as an exercise by which you can test your understanding of the original literary work. Then, compare your essays to those that follow, noting discrepancies between the two. If your essays appear lacking, that might indicate that you need to re-read the original literary work or re-familiarize yourself with the major characters.

# Aeneas

Aeneas is the protagonist, or main character, of the *Aeneid*. He is the son of Anchises, a Trojan prince, and Venus, the goddess of love. Virgil portrays Aeneas as a Trojan hero; a warrior who will lead his people to safety, found a new Trojan state, and establish order in his and his countryman's lives. Aeneas is the embodiment of Roman virtues: He is the dutiful servant of fate and of the gods, he is an exemplary leader of his people, and he is a devoted father and son. He demonstrates appropriate *pietas*—devotion to one's family, country, and mission. Aeneas's character possesses human qualities as well. He is presented as a flawed mortal man—a man with feelings.

In his role as dutiful servant of fate and of the gods, Aeneas never loses sight of his goal. Aeneas is "a man apart, devoted to his mission, a dedicated man." He tells Dido that he is "duty-bound." Aeneas faces adversity without ever losing faith in the will of fate. For example, his faith is reinforced when he sees the temple Dido built to honor Juno, "Here for the first time he took heart to hope / For safety, and to trust his destiny more / Even in affliction." In Book II, Aeneas and the Trojans perform funeral rites for Polydorus and Aeneas seeks counsel from the gods when the Trojans are leaving a country and when they arrive at a new one. Aeneas receives Apollos's prophecies through other gods. For example, the Penatës, or Trojan hearth gods, tell Aeneas to sail for Italy, the Harpies's leader, Celaeno, speaks about Apollo's instructions to her to tell his future, and Helenus also receives his revelation from Apollo. After hearing the prophecies, Aeneas is determined to fulfill his mission despite obstacles that might hinder his progress.

Throughout Book VI, Virgil reinforces that Aeneas's future is fated despite the hardships he must endure along the way. To enter the underworld, Aeneas must present a golden bough from a tree, which he can do "easily, if you are called by fate." Aeneas breaks a bough from a tree without difficulty. Later in Book X, Aeneas is described as "the God-fearing captain" because his aim with his spear is steady. Because Aeneas is submissive to the gods, he will win in battle and will ultimately reach his goal—to build a city where he and his fellow countrymen can live peaceful, ordered lives.

Aeneas easily fulfills the patriotic role as leader of his people. He provides for his people when they find a safe harbor on the North African coast of Libya by making sure they have food to eat, and he comforts and motivates them by reminding them of their destined homeland. In Book III, Aeneas becomes more comfortable with his role as leader. When he is in Thrace, Aeneas tells, "I plotted out / On that curved shore the walls of a colony—/ Though fate opposed it—and I devised the name / Aeneadae for the people, my own." By dividing the land into homesteads, Aeneas attempts to bring order and security to his people. Even though Polydorus advises Aeneas to leave Thrace, he first consults other leaders of the people before making a decision; he does not abuse his power.

Aeneas's people never question his judgment; they consistently acquiesce to his decisions, for example, during the athletic games when Aeneas declares Euryalus the winner of the foot race in spite of Salius being tripped by Nisus. Aeneas gives gifts to all the participants and exhibits his savvy as a leader by saying all the right things at the right time. When the Trojans reach Lavinia, Aeneas continues to act as the good ruler. He sends gifts to Latinus and makes plans for a new orderly city. All he asks Latinus for is "A modest settlement of the gods of home, / A strip of coast that will bring harm to no one, / Air and water, open and free to all." Virgil portrays Aeneas and his people as peaceful.

In Book IX, when Aeneas is away in Pallenteum, his spirit and leadership controls the warriors under his command. Even in his absence, his rule is respected. Aeneas, a brave warrior, never allows his emotions to cloud his sense of duty. He realizes that as leader of his people, he must fight Turnus so he can provide his people with a new city they can call their own.

The role of the good father and son is evident in Aeneas's character. Virgil describes him in Book I as "father Aeneas" and "fond father, as always thoughtful of his son." Aeneas is deeply respectful of his father and is devoted to his son. During the fall of Troy, Aeneas carries his father on his back and holds his son's hand as they make their way to the rendezvous point. In Book III, Aeneas's paternal responsibilities are expanded to include his son, the Trojans in his care, and the future of the Roman race.

Aeneas celebrates the anniversary of his father's death by making sacrifices to the gods and holding athletic games. He maintains a deep respect for his father even after Anchises's death. When Aeneas visits the underworld, the *pietas* he has for Anchises is evident. His father, returning his love and respect, asks Aeneas, "Have you at last come, has that loyalty / Your father counted on conquered the journey?" Later the notion of *pietas* is evident in Aeneas's son who assumes responsibility for rousing the warriors. He respects Aeneas's role as leader and makes every attempt to follow through with Aeneas's duties. The love that exists between fathers and sons, the ideal of *pietas*, is perhaps the most emotional bond portrayed in the *Aeneid*.

Virgil endows Aeneas with human qualities, portraying him a flawed mortal man. In Book I, he experiences overwhelming grief when he cannot find his wife Creusa during the fall of Troy and he feels discouragement when his fleet is struck by a storm. In Book II, Aeneas is uncertain about the course of action he should take. Later in Book IV, Aeneas is torn between his love for Dido and his need to fulfill his mission.

Throughout the *Aeneid*, we see Aeneas as a sensitive, compassionate man. He is sympathetic and loving towards his people. Aeneas exhibits deep feelings for humanity.

# Dido

Dido is the queen of Carthage. Virgil portrays her as Aeneas's equal and feminine counterpart. She is an antagonist, a strong, determined, and independent woman who possesses heroic dimensions. Like Aeneas, Dido fled her homeland because of circumstances beyond her control. She leads her people out of Tyre and founds Carthage. She embodies the qualities of a leader that Aeneas respects and hopes to employ when he founds Rome. She rules the Carthaginians fairly and justly, thereby maintaining order. Like Aeneas's character, Dido's character represents the best of her race.

Because Juno and Venus manipulate Dido and Aeneas, Dido becomes infatuated with Aeneas. She neglects the building projects that are underway in Carthage and the city's defense is not maintained. Virgil warns that love out of control can cause disorder, both physically and emotionally. He notes, "What good are shrines and vows to maddened lovers? / The inward fire eats the soft marrow away, / And the internal wound bleeds on in silence." Dido proves Virgil's comment when she lashes out at the gods. She lacks faith in the gods and in destiny—portraying symptoms of psychological madness. Unfortunately for Dido, her relationship with Aeneas is fated to end tragically, partly because Juno and Venus interfere and partly because Aeneas must continue on his journey to fulfill his destiny.

In Book IV, Dido knows that her relationship with Aeneas is fated to fail. She realizes that her love/lust for Aeneas is her downfall; however, she is unable to change the course of events. She asks herself, "What am I saying? Where am I? What madness / Takes me out of myself? Dido poor soul, / Your evil doing has come home to you."

Virgil compares Dido's uncontrolled passion to a consuming fire that can not be extinguished: "The queen, for her part, all that evening ached / With longing that her heart's blood fed, a wound / Or inward fire eating her away." Later, when she discovers that Aeneas plans to leave Carthage, she becomes "all aflame / With rage." Fittingly, Dido dies on a pyre used for burning corpses in funeral rites by committing suicide with Aeneas's sword. Her suicide, an act of courage, proves she is a tragic, as well as a romantic heroine.

# Turnus

Turnus is a prince of the Rutulian tribe and the leader of the Latin forces who oppose the settlement of the Trojans in Latium. Like Aeneas, he is a physically superior warrior. He is Aeneas's antagonist, his chief enemy, and heroic counterpart.

Turnus's character as antagonist serves a similar purpose in the second half of *The Aeneid* as did Dido's character in the first half. Turnus's militant fury is the counterpart to Dido's erotic fury. Like Dido, Turnus is an individualist who follows his own will to the point of excess, and he is opposed in spirit to Aeneas who is dutiful and self-sacrificing. Intense pride and a desire for personal fame are Turnus's motivation. When he is aroused by the fury, Allecto, to stage war between the Latins and Trojans, thereby forestalling destiny (the settlement of the Trojans in Latium and Aeneas's marriage to Lavinia), Turnus's character flaws become evident. He is linked with disorder. He has a passion for war, and unlike Aeneas, he has a lust for bloodshed. Turnus "raised the flag of war," and instigates chaos amongst the people, "Then hearts were stirred by fear, then all of Latium / Joined in distracted tumult, and young men / Grew bloody-minded, wild."

Turnus is portrayed as "the rash prince" who lacks control. For example, after gaining entrance to the Trojans's camp, he passionately slaughters his enemies, consumed with his lust for blood. Blinded by his passion and lack of control, Turnus bypasses an opportunity to admit his troops to the Trojan camp and claim a decisive victory. Virgil notes: "And if the thought had come to the champion / To break the gate-bars, to admit his friends, / That would have been the last day of the war, /

The last for Trojans. But high rage and mindless / Lust for slaughter drove the passionate man / Against his enemies." Turnus's reckless behavior prevents him from accomplishing what should have been his primary concern, defeat of the Trojans and marriage to Lavinia.

The violence in Book IX enables Virgil to portray the depravity, or corruptness, of Turnus's character. He appears to have no sense of justice or of what is morally acceptable as he flaunts the death of Nisus and Euryalus by marching amongst the people with their heads stuck atop spears.

In Book XII, Turnus's lack of control reaches its climax. Turnus is unable to control his emotional rage. His passion is described as "hot and unquenchable." Virgil compares Turnus's passion for Lavinia to that of Dido for Aeneas in the first half of *The Aeneid*. The more Turnus craves Lavinia, the more he wants to do battle. It becomes evident that Turnus's lack of emotional control clouds his military judgment. Virgil notes, "He did not know himself. His knees gave way, / His blood ran cold and froze."

Turnus's is the anti-hero, the character who, because of his disreputable behavior, is fated to die. His character behaves in a manner inferior to Aeneas's character. He defames the sanctity of death by stepping on Pallas's body after killing him and he acts dishonorably by removing the swordbelt from the dead man's body. Virgil comments on Turnus's behavior, "The minds of men are ignorant of fate / And of their future lot, unskilled to keep / Due measure when some triumph sets them high. / For Turnus there will come a time / When he would give the world to see again / An untouched Pallas, and will hate this day, / Hate that belt taken." Because Turnus's future has been sealed by fate, he dies as a result of his actions and Aeneas, and civic virtue, triumphs.

# CRITICAL
# ESSAYS

On the pages that follow, the writer of this study guide provides critical scholarship on various aspects of Virgil's *Aeneid*. These interpretive essays are in-tended solely to enhance your understanding of the original literary work; they are supplemental materials and are not to replace your reading of *Aeneid*. When you're finished reading *Aeneid*, and prior to your reading this study guide's critical essays, consider making a bulleted list of what you think are the most important themes and symbols. Write a short paragraph under each bullet explaining why you think that theme or symbol is important; include at least one short quote from the original literary work that supports your contention. Then, test your list and reasons against those found in the following essays. Do you include themes and symbols that the study guide author doesn't? If so, this self test might indicate that you are well on your way to understanding original literary work. But if not, perhaps you will need to re-read *Aeneid*.

# Literary Predecessors of the *Aeneid*

Although Virgil lived and wrote two thousand years ago, he was the heir to a literary and cultural tradition that was many centuries older. A master of his art and a great creative genius, it is both understandable and natural that the form and content of the *Aeneid* were influenced by other writers. Among these influential sources are Homer, the *Cyclic Epics*, Euripides, Alexandrian poets, and earlier Roman writers.

The foremost influence on Virgil was Homer, the Greek poet who composed the *Iliad* and the *Odyssey*. By Virgil's time, Homer was acknowledged as the greatest of all poets, and Virgil studied Homeric epic poetry in order to develop his own artistic techniques. Writing the *Aeneid*, Virgil consciously competed against Homer, for he was composing what he hoped would become the national poem of the Roman people, just as the Homeric epics were of such special significance to the Greeks.

From Homer, Virgil derived many of the technical characteristics of the *Aeneid*, such as the use of hexameter verse, in which each poetic line consists of six metrical feet, each foot having two syllables; the twelve-book division of epic poetry; and the use of epithets. However, the two poets's attitudes toward the world vary greatly. The Homeric epics are works in praise of the greatness and nobility of rugged individualism, whereas the *Aeneid* preaches the priority of organized society and the state over its citizens in order for individuals to achieve happiness. There is much to commend in both attitudes, and both poets express their views in works of great beauty.

Virgil strove to duplicate many of the famous episodes in the *Iliad* and the *Odyssey* in order to surpass Homer's literary reputation. Additionally, he wanted to demonstrate that Latin was as well adapted to poetry as Greek.

The first half of the *Aeneid* resembles the first half of the *Odyssey*, which, because that poem has twice as many divisions as Virgil's epic, comprises the twelve books that concern the wanderings of Odysseus as he seeks his homeland of Ithaca. The two heroes sail the same seas, and in Book III of the *Aeneid*, Virgil brings Aeneas and his people into contact with some of the same perils, thus providing strong reminders of the earlier epic.

In addition, the *Aeneid*'s second half, which begins with Book VII, bears a likeness to the *Odyssey*'s second half: Aeneas's struggle to establish the Trojans in Italy recalls how Odysseus forced out his wife Penelope's suitors, who usurped his place in his own household during his absence. Without any doubt, however, the *Aeneid*'s last six books, particularly starting with Book IX, when war finally breaks out, more strongly resemble the *Iliad*. One example of this similarity is the comparison between Turnus, who fights against the Trojans during Aeneas's absence, and Hector, the Trojan prince who engages the Greeks in the absence of Achilles, who, angry with Agamemnon for having taken the woman Briseis from him, refuses to participate in the war until fairly late in Homer's epic. Achilles eventually returns to battle and slays Hector in order to avenge the death of his friend Patroclus at the hands of the Trojan hero, just as Aeneas slays Turnus in order to avenge Pallas's death at the hands of the Rutulian prince.

Many of the dreams, prophecies, and lists of genealogies in the *Aeneid* evoke Homer's works. For example, Aeneas's dream of Hector on the night that Troy falls to the Greeks recalls Achilles's vision, in Book XXIII of the *Iliad*, of the great warrior Patroclus, who, having been slain by Hector, implores Achilles to perform the funeral rites necessary for his passage into the underworld. Patroclus visits Achilles because he is driven by a profound personal concern, while Hector's appearance, like other incidents in the *Aeneid* that are based on Homer, is full of patriotic import. This parallel between Hector's and Patroclus's appearances is the only significant reference in the *Aeneid*'s Book II to Homer, who could not have influenced Virgil's description of Troy's fall for the simple reason that his *Iliad* ends with the funeral of Hector, before Troy is destroyed, while his *Odyssey* begins ten years after the war is over.

It should be noted, however, that Homer was thoroughly learned in the stories having to do with Troy's fall, particularly the wooden horse, which is referred to three times in the *Odyssey*—by Helen and Menelaus in Book IV, when Telemachus, Odysseus's son, visits them at Sparta while seeking news of his absent father; by the blind bard Demodocus in the presence of Odysseus, who is being entertained with tales of the Trojan War in the king of Phaeacia's court in Book VIII; and finally by Odysseus himself when, in Book XI, he speaks to Achilles's ghost in the underworld about the bravery of his son Pyrrhus, who, as one of the warriors hidden in the wooden horse, showed no fear while waiting to be sprung from the horse's body cavity.

Nowhere is Homer more easily recognized as Virgil's chief source of poetic reference than in Book VI of the *Aeneid*. The story of Aeneas's descent into the underworld abounds in details that reflect original counterparts in Book XI of the *Odyssey*, which tells of Odysseus's own visit to the land of the dead to consult the ghost of the Theban seer Tiresias, who resembles Anchises in his prophetic role. However, Anchises's philosophical concepts, which prepare for the historical pageant that is central to Book VI, have absolutely no place in the *Odyssey*, being alien to Homer's joyous, life-embracing realism. Anchises's presenting Rome's glorious future is entirely different from Tiresias's role, which is to advise Odysseus only on the events of the hero's own future before and after arriving home in Ithaca.

Here, as elsewhere, Virgil's main reason for constructing parallels to Homer, which he was no doubt certain his readers would identify and relish, was to add luster to the *Aeneid* as a latter-day epic appearing in another language more than seven centuries after his immensely prestigious, literary forebear. Virgil gives Homer's original incidents an import for the development of his own epic that is absent from the *Iliad* and the *Odyssey*. Never far from his mind is his purpose of making the *Aeneid* a national epic (discussed in the next essay), which neither of Homer's works were. Once we understand how Virgil adapted his borrowings from Homer for his own ends, we see how far he was from being a mere imitator of the great poet who preceded him.

In the centuries that immediately followed the time of Homer, a number of epics of little quality were written that supplemented the information in the *Iliad* and the *Odyssey*. These poems, known as the *Cyclic Epics*, describe the events of the Trojan War before and after the period covered by the *Iliad* and recount the additional adventures of other heroes besides Odysseus. Only fragments of these minor epics survive today, but scholars have a fairly good idea of their entire contents. The *Cyclic Epics* provided Virgil with a wealth of mythological material, which he incorporated into the *Aeneid* in order to enrich his poem. The most important portions of the *Aeneid* to be drawn from these minor poems are the stories of the wooden horse and the sack of Troy, which are dramatically retold in Book II.

For Greek tragedians who wrote in the fifth and fourth centuries B.C., their favorite source of plots was their mythological heritage, and, naturally, the Trojan War was a major part of this tradition. Many playwrights dealt with incidents drawn from Homer or the *Cyclic* poets, and Virgil, being a scholar as well as an artist, was thoroughly acquainted with these dramatists, including Sophocles and Aeschylus. The plays of the Greek dramatist Euripides especially influenced him, for Virgil possesses the same humanistic outlook and horror of war that Euripides was renowned for. Euripides's *Trojan Women* and *Hecuba*, which question one of the most pathetic situations of any war—the fate of noncombatants who, through no fault of their own, must suffer bitter hardships and endure the loss of home, family, pride, and country—must have been on Virgil's mind when he wrote about the fate of the Trojans in Book II. No doubt Virgil recalled Euripides's *Andromachë* when he described Aeneas's encounter with Andromachë, Hector's widow, at Buthrotum in Book III, by which time she had become Helenus's wife.

By the third century B.C., the center of Hellenic culture and scholarship had moved from mainland Greece to the city of Alexandria, Egypt. Here, a school of poetry developed that is noted for its love of learning, literary decoration, and stylistic polish. Virgil and many of his Roman compatriots were deeply and permanently influenced by this school's methods. One of the most important poets of this period was Apollonius of Rhodes, who composed the *Argonautica*, an epic in four books that concerns the quest for the Golden Fleece. A comparison of the romance of Jason and Medea in the *Argonautica* to that of Aeneas and Dido in the *Aeneid*, and the treatment of the gods in both poems clearly indicate Virgil's debt to Apollonius.

Like most Romans, Virgil was subject to the sway of Greek culture and Greek philosophy. For example, Plato, whose imaginative speculations concern the nature of the soul and its fate after death, influenced the *Aeneid*'s Book VI, in which Aeneas visits his father in the underworld. Nonetheless, Virgil wrote in the Latin language and was the product of a Roman environment. His education, like that of all well-off Romans, was predominantly Greek, but Rome had its own long and fruitful literary history, which he was also familiar with.

Among Roman writers, Virgil learned most from Ennius, an epic poet of the second century B.C., who composed the *Annales*, a poem tracing Rome's history from Aeneas's wanderings to Ennius's own time; Lucretius, a poet of the early first century B.C., who wrote *On the Nature of Things*, a philosophical epic from which Virgil derived many of his own philosophical ideas; and Catullus, a lyric poet who lived in Julius Caesar's time. Each of these Roman writers was himself under the influence of Greek literary models, just as Virgil was.

Discovering the many sources from which Virgil drew ideas in no way lessens the magnitude of his achievement. A student of his predecessors but never a mere imitator, he reshaped, unified, and gave new meaning to his borrowings. His genius is shown by the beauty and originality of the *Aeneid*, which has become the literary justification and explanation of the Roman Empire to the entire world.

# The *Aeneid* as a National Epic

Less concerned with the life and adventures of Aeneas than with the part he played in founding the Roman state, the *Aeneid* is a national epic, a glorification and exaltation of Rome and its people. Virgil has a spiritualized, idealistic, and aspiring conception of Rome, which he views as majestic and sacred, ordained by destiny to rule the world. He saw a golden age of human life emerging during Augustus's reign, a golden age brought about by the gods. The *Aeneid* is designed to exalt this new, ordered society and to glorify its virtues and finest features by their personification in Aeneas, an epic hero who is meant to represent the archetypal Roman. Aeneas embodies the most important Roman personal qualities and attributes, particularly the Roman sense of duty and responsibility that Virgil thought of as having built the Rome he loved.

During the century prior to Augustus's rule, the Roman republic was ravaged by a constant series of civil wars, which caused large human and financial losses. Finally, under Augustus, the state was unified once again. With the restoration of peace and order, and with the government taking an active interest in many different phases of economic and social life, Rome regained its prosperity and happiness. Unfortunately, this return to order was brought about through the establishment of an imperial form of government. While peace was restored, many of the old liberties that Romans had become accustomed to were abandoned, a situation that caused serious problems and occupied the minds of many responsible citizens, including Virgil.

In the *Aeneid*, Virgil evaluates the new conditions under which Romans live. His epic poem enumerates the most worthwhile features of both republican and imperial Rome and treats the two together as if they were a single, intertwined whole. This unity implies that the glories of one form of government are the glories of the other, an argument that weakened the belief that the empire under Augustus was a new and foreign political entity. Furthermore, through prophecies, Virgil indicates in many ways that the imperial period is destined to be a new golden age for Rome: Only now, during the Augustan Age, can all of the Roman people's noblest aspirations and hopes be fulfilled.

By writing the *Aeneid*, Virgil hoped to extol the virtues of Augustus in a literary fashion that would last forever. Unlike the *Iliad* and the

*Odyssey*, which are oral epics, the *Aeneid* is a literary epic, composed in writing and intended to be read by an audience of literate people who live in a settled, civilized society. All epic poetry has a serious theme narrated on a grand scale and intended to heighten the understanding of human nature and the meaning of life, but in a literary epic, the ideological content is more important than the human story itself. A comparison of the *Aeneid* and the *Iliad*, for example, shows that literary epic is more didactic; it subordinates its human characters and their affairs to its philosophical and moral themes.

Most important, the purposes of oral and literary epics are greatly distinct, a difference that has a profound effect on the epics's contents and the ways in which their stories develop. Oral epic was intended primarily to provide diversion and entertainment to its audience, although it also embodied much of the history and folk-wisdom of the culture in which it was created. For example, although the *Iliad* has a serious theme with many important moral lessons, these teachings are only a by-product of Achilles's story, which is the main reason for the poem's existence. Literary epic, on the other hand, always has a didactic purpose that is foremost in the poet's mind when he composes his work. Poems like the *Aeneid* communicate serious philosophical, moral, and patriotic messages that subordinate their narrative stories. Because of this subordination, literary epic has a higher degree of unity and coherence than oral epic, but its human characters are less believable and oftentimes less admirable in human terms, for they lack many important human qualities. To the poet and his readers, the underlying national theme is the epic's main element.

Aeneas, the hero of the *Aeneid*, is plainly a personification of the most respected Roman virtues, and we are frequently reminded that Augustus is his descendent. The implication of this association between Aeneas and Augustus to Virgil's contemporary readers is clear: They would infer that Augustus shares many of his ancestor Aeneas's fine qualities; their full confidence in the emperor's judgment would be justified; and they would be foolhardy and pretentious to criticize Augustus's new government.

During his wanderings, Aeneas undergoes many hardships. In every instance, he consoles himself by remembering the great destiny of the empire that he is fated to found. With this knowledge to strengthen him, he constantly subordinates his own desires to his dream of a new Rome, an attitude that set an impressive example for many Romans. Aeneas's many personal sacrifices taught Roman citizens that their own personal doubts or complaints about Augustus's government were of little importance compared to the welfare and the needs of society. Individuals had to submerge their petty grievances for the good of all; a strong and centralized state was the only guarantee for peace and unity.

Romans also would have been comforted to know that the *Aeneid*'s gods and goddesses were concerned with Rome's future. Troy's fall is a grave defeat for the Trojans, but it is a necessary condition for the evolution of Rome, which, according to the poem, is destined to become Troy's successor in the far distant future. The exultation of the gods, Jupiter among them, as they behold Troy's collapse in Book II does not contradict the belief that, as a group, they are on the Trojans's side. At times, Venus speaks with the voice of a prudent Roman matron, and even Juno is on her way to becoming reconciled to the Trojans's presence in Italy. In any case, Virgil's Roman contemporaries had only to point to their own unending series of successes in order to demonstrate to their satisfaction that Rome and its empire had permanently won divine favor.

Convinced by Virgil's arguments in the *Aeneid*, many members of Rome's educated class ceased their opposition to Augustus and grew accustomed to their emperor's government. Meanwhile, the *Aeneid* became a standard school text. Every new generation of students was exposed to Virgil's epic poem, and from it developed an unselfish dedication to the Roman imperial ideal. Thus, besides being a literary masterpiece, the *Aeneid* became what was, perhaps, the strongest intellectual bulwark of the Roman Empire.

# CliffsNotes Review

Use this CliffsNotes Review to test your understanding of the original text, and reinforce what you've learned in this book. After you work through the review and essay questions, and the fun and useful practice projects, you're well on your way to understanding a comprehensive and meaningful interpretation of Virgil's *Aeneid*.

## Q&A

1. The *Aeneid*'s opening book incorporates a literary device known as _____.

2. In addition to Aeneas, perhaps the most important figure in the first half of the epic poem is _____.

3. _____ is queen of the gods and Jupiter's wife.

4. In Book III, _____ and his fellow Cyclopes attack the Trojans when they land near Mount Aetna.

5. _____ throws open the gates of Mar's temple, thereby signifying the beginning of the war between the Trojans and the Latins.

**Answers:** (1) *in media res*. (2) Dido. (3) Juno. (4) Polyphemus. (5) Janus.

## Essay Questions

1. Discuss the nature of fate and how it operates in the epic poem.

2. What esteemed Roman virtues are embodied in Aeneas?

3. Compare Aeneas and Dido. Is Dido as grand a figure as Aeneas? Why or why not?

4. Compare Venus's and Juno's reasons for wanting to see Aeneas and Dido married. Why does Aeneas and Dido's love affair, which Juno surprisingly favors, actually defeat the queen of the gods's purpose in the long run?

5. What do Lausus's and Pallas's deaths signify?

6. Compare Priam, Troy's king, to Latinus. Are both ineffective rulers, or are their desires to strike peace with their respective foes admirable?

**7.** Discuss the nature and function of the gods and goddesses. In what ways do they resemble human beings? Do you find any of them admirable?

**8.** Why does Virgil end the *Aeneid*, a national epic, with a dark, gloomy description of the death of Turnus, the Trojans's major mortal enemy?

# Practice Projects

**1.** Create a world map showing Aeneas's oceanic voyage from the Ionian Sea through the Mediterranean Sea to the Tyrrhenian Sea.

**2.** Dido and Turnus both play important roles in the epic poem. Along with other readers, debate which character is more tragic. Support your debate points with passages from the poem.

**3.** Design a Web site devoted to the *Aeneid*. Include links to other sites for historical, social, and informational material that would help readers better understand Virgil's time.

**4.** Take on the persona of one of the characters and write a short essay introducing yourself to others. What motivates you? What are your goals?

# CliffsNotes Resource Center

The learning doesn't need to stop here. CliffsNotes Resource Center shows you the best of the best—links to the best information in print and online about the poet and/or related works. And don't think that this is all we've prepared for you; we've put all kinds of pertinent information at www.cliffsnotes.com. Look for all the terrific resources at your favorite bookstore or local library and on the Internet. When you're online, make your first stop www.cliffsnotes.com where you'll find more incredibly useful information about Virgil's *Aeneid*.

## Books

This CliffsNotes book provides a meaningful interpretation of Virgil's *Aeneid*. If you are looking for information about the poet and/or related works, check out these other publications:

*A Day in Old Rome: A Picture of Roman Life,* by William Sterns Davis, is a description of Roman life including the city, street life, homes, Roman women and marriage, clothing, food and drink, courts and laws, religion, and other aspects of life. New York: Biblio and Tannen, 1966.

*The Art of Vergil,* by Victor Poschl, explores the basic themes of the *Aeneid*, as well as principal figures (Aeneas, Dido, and Turnus), symbolism, and mood. Ann Arbor: University of Michigan Press, 1962.

*Larousse Encyclopedia of Mythology,* is a comprehensive "Who's Who" of the better known gods, goddesses, heroes, demons, angels, and saints from all over the world. New York: Prometheus Press, 1959.

*Religion in Virgil,* by Cyril Bailey, is a detailed examination of religious ideas and practices evident in Virgil's poems. Oxford: Clarendon Press, 1935.

*The Roman Way,* by Edith Hamilton, is a portrayal of Roman qualities as seen by great authors. New York: W.W. Norton, 1993.

*Vergil's Italy,* by Alexander G. McKay, discusses Virgil's achievement as a poet in detail. The author includes characterization, Virgil's poetic method, a discussion of the *Aeneid*, the use of particular regions in Virgil's writings, and social and political factors as experienced by Virgil. Connecticut: New York Graphic Society, 1968.

*Virgil,* by F.J.H. Letters, is a study of Virgil's poetry including an explanation of his style and method. New York: Sheed & Ward, 1946.

*Virgil,* by T.R. Glover, includes the author's picture of Virgil that developed during five years of lectures to students. This comprehensive work includes background information about Virgil, literary influences on Virgil, Virgil's contemporaries, the myths of Aeneas, information about Italy and Rome, an interpretation about life that centers on Dido, Aeneas, Hades, and Olympus. New York: Macmillan, 1930.

It's easy to find books published by Wiley Publishing, Inc. You'll find them in your favorite bookstores (on the Internet and at a store near you). We also have three Web sites that you can use to read about all the books we publish:

- www.cliffsnotes.com
- www.dummies.com
- www.wiley.com

# Internet

Check out these Web resources for more information about Virgil and the *Aeneid*:

**The Age of Fable: Chapter XXXI: Adventures of Aeneas, the Harpies, Dido, and Palinurus**, http://www.showgate.com/medea/bulfinch/bull31.html—features a description of Aeneas's journey, including his confrontation with the Harpies, relationship with Dido, and relationship with Palinurus. This site includes many links that provide details of significant events.

**Welcome to the World of the Aeneid**, http://members.tripod.com/~Chaipo—features a brief summary of the epic along with a list of sites related to the *Aeneid*, Virgil, and the Romans.

Next time you're on the Internet, don't forget to drop by www.cliffsnotes.com. We created an online Resource Center that you can use today, tomorrow, and beyond.

# Send Us Your Favorite Tips

In your quest for knowledge, have you ever experienced that sublime moment when you figure out a trick that saves time or trouble? Perhaps you realized you were taking ten steps to accomplish something that could have taken two. Or you found a little-known workaround that achieved great results. If you've discovered a useful tip that helped you understand Virgil's *Aeneid* and you'd like to share

it, the CliffsNotes staff would love to hear from you. Go to our Web site at
www.cliffsnotes.com and click the Talk to Us button. If we select your tip, we
may publish it as part of CliffsNotes Daily, our exciting, free e-mail newsletter. To
find out more or to subscribe to a newsletter, go to www.cliffsnotes.com on the
Web.

# Index